PENGUIN BOOKS

BIG CAPITAL

Anna Minton is a writer, journalist and Reader in Architecture at the University of East London. Her first book, *Ground Control*, was published in 2009 to widespread acclaim. The Royal Commission's Fellow in the Built Environment between 2011 and 2014, she is a regular contributor to the *Guardian* and a frequent broadcaster and commentator. She lives in South London with her partner and their two sons.

ANNA MINTON

Big Capital

Who is London For?

PENGUIN BOOKS

PENGUIN BOOKS

UK | USA | Canada | Ireland | Australia
India | New Zealand | South Africa

Penguin Books is part of the Penguin Random House group of companies
whose addresses can be found at global.penguinrandomhouse.com

Penguin
Random House
UK

First published 2017
001

Copyright © Anna Minton, 2017
Photographs copyright © Henrietta Williams, 2017

The moral right of the author has been asserted

Set in 9.25/12.5 pt Sabon LT Std
Typeset by Jouve (UK), Milton Keynes
Printed in Great Britain by Clays Ltd, St Ives plc

A CIP catalogue record for this book is available from the British Library

ISBN: 978-0-141-98499-5

For all those who shared
their stories about the housing crisis with me

Contents

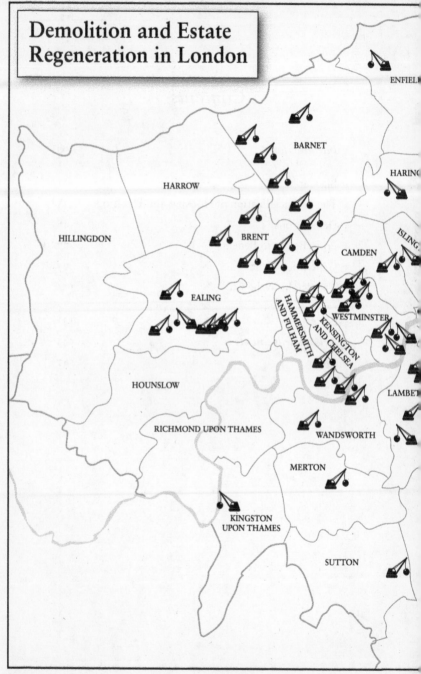

Demolition and Estate Regeneration in London

ENFIEL

BARNET

HARING

HARROW

HILLINGDON

BRENT

CAMDEN

ISLING

EALING

HAMMERSMITH AND FULHAM

KENSINGTON AND CHELSEA

WESTMINSTER

HOUNSLOW

LAMBET

RICHMOND UPON THAMES

WANDSWORTH

MERTON

KINGSTON UPON THAMES

SUTTON

Disclaimer: it is not possible to provide an entirely accurate map, as different schemes are at different stages of the planning process. Sources: Concrete Action; Architects for Social Housing; Agnes Chandler.

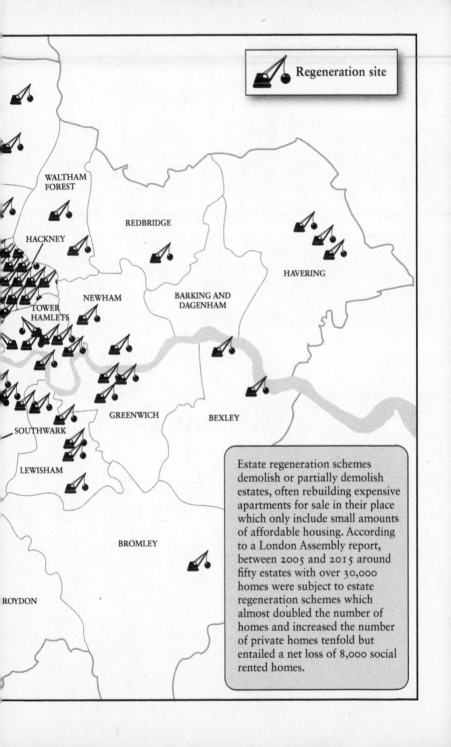

Regeneration site

WALTHAM FOREST

REDBRIDGE

HACKNEY

HAVERING

NEWHAM

BARKING AND DAGENHAM

TOWER HAMLETS

GREENWICH

BEXLEY

SOUTHWARK

LEWISHAM

BROMLEY

ROYDON

Estate regeneration schemes demolish or partially demolish estates, often rebuilding expensive apartments for sale in their place which only include small amounts of affordable housing. According to a London Assembly report, between 2005 and 2015 around fifty estates with over 30,000 homes were subject to estate regeneration schemes which almost doubled the number of homes and increased the number of private homes tenfold but entailed a net loss of 8,000 social rented homes.

Introduction

'Surrounded by boxes yet again, about to move knowing that we will be moving again in the new year. I have cleaned and painted the new flat and it's still a dump with damp patches and a moth eaten carpet throughout. I am forty-six and I have lived in over thirty houses and I still have no security.' This was posted on social media at the end of 2016 by Jan. She has a good job earning almost £40,000 a year, her husband works full time, they have two children and this is what they have to put up with. These are some of the replies her post elicited, none of which registered surprise: 'Truly a tragedy isn't it. Other countries so different.' 'It's so tough. I have a work capability assessment on Monday that could lead to issues with my benefits . . . and therefore my rent. No security either . . . exhausting.' 'What a nightmare. There is nothing more destroying to peace of mind than moving because you have to. I moved a number of times last year before getting to Berlin. I'm lucky that I have this place now but living in another country with another language is not necessarily a dream to chase.' 'The current situation is broken isn't it. Unless it's sorted out quickly very few people will get through.'

In the adverts on the hoardings all over the city is another London, populated by smart-looking people and luxury balcony apartments. This is the destination of choice for foreign investors and the new global elite of oligarchs, billionaires and the super-rich who make up the so-called 'alpha elites', who are attracted by the UK's very favourable tax environment. Entire neighbourhoods in the 'alpha' parts of London – St John's Wood, Highgate, Hampstead, Notting Hill Gate, Kensington, to name but a few – have changed out of all recognition over the last decade. Estate agents refer to these centrally located 'super prime' areas as the 'golden postcodes'. They have long been wealthy places, home to monied communities from all over the world as well as the English upper classes, but in the past, like most of London, they were also mixed areas. Now even the wealthy are displaced from Kensington by multimillionaire 'Ultra High Net Worth Individuals', who in turn displace others from central London to suburban areas, creating a domino effect that ripples out through the city, with the consequence that average-income earners and the poor move to the periphery or out of the capital altogether, placing pressure on housing and prices around the country.

Simultaneously, London's much-loved skyline is being transformed by one of the greatest waves of new construction seen in the city, with no fewer than 300 planned luxury residential towers going up. Nine Elms, a huge development which stretches from Lambeth Bridge to Chelsea Bridge, will be home to the luxury Battersea Power Station Complex, the new US embassy and Embassy Gardens, which, with its Sky Pool suspended ten storeys up in the air between two luxury tower blocks, is at the pinnacle of new London: a playground for the rich, built on an inhuman scale. From Nine Elms up to Vauxhall and along to Southwark and Blackfriars bridges, mile upon mile of serried ranks of balconied apartments in gated complexes have already been built and at Elephant and Castle the Australian property developer Lendlease is working with Southwark Council to render the area unrecognizable, replacing with a forest of luxury towers the affordable housing which once characterized the area. Outside some of these buildings 'anti-homeless spikes' prohibit homeless people from sitting or sleeping on the pavement.

Since 2008 much has been written about the housing crisis. Exploring the fallout from that year's financial crash, which combined large increases in wealth in property assets for the richest with widespread austerity, *Big Capital* makes explicit the links between the sheer wealth at the top and the housing crisis, which does not affect just those at the bottom but the majority of Londoners who struggle to buy properties and pay extortionate rents. From the removal from their homes of people on low incomes to the use of property purely as profit and no longer as a social good, the active flouting of democracy by business and local councils alike, the scandal in housing benefit and the pressure on individuals and families at all income levels, this is a new politics of space. Replacing the politics of class, these trends are not limited to London. The same circuits of global capital are also transforming San Francisco, New York and Vancouver in North America, European cities from Berlin to Barcelona and towns and cities in the UK, from Bristol to Manchester and Margate to Hastings. This has led to a constant hum of debate about the impacts of that much misunderstood term 'gentrification'. But this isn't gentrification, it's another phenomenon entirely. The flood of global capital is being allowed to reconfigure the country.

'Gentrification' is one of those terms, rather like 'affordable housing', that lost its real meaning long ago. It was first coined in 1964 by the sociologist Ruth Glass, who used it to describe the changes taking place in Islington, as middle-class families moved into old working-class homes and did them up, creating desirable Victorian residences. 'One by one, many of the working class quarters of London have been invaded by the middle classes . . . Once this process of "gentrification" starts in a district, it goes on rapidly until all or most of the original working class occupiers are displaced, and the whole social character of the district is changed,' she wrote. Fifteen years ago the academic Loretta Lees wrote about 'super gentrification' to describe the impact of the new class of finance professionals in New York and parts of London such as Barnsbury and Notting Hill Gate. Although it has always been a contested term, 'gentrification' adopted positive connotations associated with improving areas. But the speed of capital flows into places between the 1960s and the early 2000s bears no comparison to what is happening today. The rate of return on London property, even in a market slowed by economic uncertainty, far exceeds growth, let alone wages, which are among the lowest in Europe. It is these rates of return on property that are driving the reconfiguration of London, boosted by policy decisions carried out by local authorities, which are in tune with deliberate changes in housing policy and the property market, designed to take maximum advantage of the attraction of London real estate to global investors. This has little to do with the process that Glass or even Lees describe, which saw capital invested in gentrifying parts of the city at a much slower rate, over generations rather than a few years: as such, it is crucial that the impact of global capital and foreign investment is scrutinized for its local effects.

The title of this book is a nod to Thomas Piketty's landmark study, *Capital in the Twenty-First Century*, which investigates the consequences for inequality when the rate of return on rent is greater than the rate of economic growth. I hope to expose the lie that the housing crisis is a market question of supply and demand. Governments of all stripes have argued that we simply need to loosen planning restrictions and build more homes for sale. It may *seem* logical enough to argue that if we increase housing supply then prices will come down and there will be more homes to go around, but the UK housing market doesn't function like a pure market: it is linked to global capital flows, not local circumstances. These global flows are distorting the market and ensuring supply is being skewed towards investors.

The UN Declaration of Human Rights includes the right to adequate housing. But in the UK housing is now, first and foremost, a financial asset, a safety deposit box for the super-rich and a cash cow for growing numbers of Russian, Middle Eastern, Asian, Chinese and some British investors. In a 2014 report, following a visit to the UK, the UN's Special Rapporteur for Housing concluded that the adequate right to housing was being eroded by cuts to benefits related to housing. As she acknowledged, it wasn't always like this. We have an internationally admired housing history which, like other cornerstones of public policy such as the NHS, was built on a welfare state superstructure created out of the horrors of the Second World War. Western governments wanted to prove to their populations that social democratic capitalist societies could also provide public goods such as hospitals and housing for all, which were available beyond the Iron Curtain alongside authoritarian government and censorship. In Britain and across the West these competing pressures kept capitalism in check. But over the last thirty years, since the fall of the Berlin Wall, unbridled capitalism in the form of a new neoliberal framework has brought the market into every aspect of public policy, in the NHS, in education and in housing, where privatization, deregulation and property speculation are now the dominant approaches. The result is a system in crisis, rife with the contradictions of two opposing ideologies – socialism and neoliberalism – combined with the unintended consequences of a market-led approach to public goods.

Public housing accounted for a huge proportion of British housing throughout the twentieth century. Since the 1980s, it has been steadily removed from the system, through the combination of Right to Buy, which saw the sell-off of 2 million council homes, and Buy to Let, which has resulted in 40 per cent of those former council homes now being owned by private landlords who rent them out for three and four times the money. During the 1980s a decision was taken to cease building housing for those on lower incomes and to create instead a system whereby housing benefit 'would take the strain'. The combination of the decision to stop building council housing and Right to Buy shifted social tenants into private rented housing. It is one of the reasons why we have such a shortage of affordable homes. But since changes to housing benefit were introduced in the late 2000s, the situation has become far more acute for people on low incomes. One of the unacknowledged links is that this change doesn't just affect those in difficult financial circumstances; it affects everybody. Linking housing benefit to the market adds inflationary pressure to rents, not just in London but all around the country (as I'll explain in chapter 4). Housing, and the different layers of society it affects, is seen as a set of separate issues when in fact it is one issue: what happens at the top affects the middle and the bottom, and vice versa, with the influx of wealth from the top displacing communities across the city, while the introduction of a market in housing benefit adds inflationary pressures on rents for everybody.

Chapter 1 investigates the role of big capital in creating the alpha parts of the city and its impact on Londoners, displacing rather than enriching local communities. Chapter 2 tracks the role of postwar housing and planning policy and the breakdown of the social contract in housing and planning which provides the context for the scandalous failure of today, where despite research showing that the profits of the top five biggest housebuilders increased by a staggering 480 per cent between 2010 and 2015, building genuinely affordable housing is rarely considered financially viable by them. Chapter 3 looks at the demolition of London's housing estates and explains why this is happening at a time when affordable housing is needed more than ever. The devastation caused to the lives of individuals and communities by the resulting wave of displacement has led to an increase in the incidence of mental health problems. This is equally a feature of chapter 4, which investigates the housing benefit crisis, which is forcing poor Londoners unable to afford current rents to move to other parts of the country; this has now become official policy in Westminster. Chapter 5 is about 'generation rent' and describes the range of problems in private rented housing, from slum landlords and 'beds in sheds' to middle-class Londoners under the age of forty-five who can no longer comfortably afford to live in the city. A generation is being affected and our essential services, such as hospitals and schools, as well as the majority of our businesses, are being undermined. Chapter 6 points towards an alternative approach based on the idea of 'the Right to the City', which provides a framework for addressing today's politics of space, based on inclusion rather than exclusion.

Increasingly, London and many other British, European and North American cities no longer serve people from a wide range of communities and income brackets, excluding them from expensive amenities and reasonably priced housing and forcing them into intolerable conditions or out of the city altogether, raising the question of who is the city for? Today, capital flowing to every aspect of land, property and housing means the whole system has opened itself up to financialization. From the market in student housing to 'super prime' properties, the result is a system failing to meet the needs of people. London is an acute example of why this is happening. What happens in this city affects everyone in Britain, both indirectly through the extreme concentration of wealth in the capital and directly as the policies and the people move through the country. It also exemplifies international trends occurring on a global scale. Why is this happening? And how can we change it, so that housing becomes about people rather than profit?

I

Big Capital

THE 'KLEPTOCRACY TOUR'

The UK is a prime destination for corrupt individuals looking
to invest or launder the proceeds of their illicit wealth, enjoy
a luxury lifestyle and cleanse their reputations.

Transparency International[1]

The instruction was given to board the coach at Victoria Embank-
ment, just around the corner from Parliament Square. I was joining
the 'Kleptocracy Tour', a bus ride with a difference around London,
led by former Russian banker turned anti-corruption activist Roman
Borisovich. The tours, timed to coincide with a UK government
anti-corruption summit in 2016, were designed to show that rather
than taking the lead in tackling the problem, London is the world
capital for corruption and money laundering, the proceeds being fun-
nelled straight into the super prime and prime property market.

This came not long after the Panama Papers, the enormous leak
of 11.5 million documents from offshore law firm Mossack Fonseca,
and it was sadly no surprise to hear that it is into London property
that global money launderers and corrupt world leaders plough their
capital, through tens of thousands of shell companies which cannot
be traced back to their original owners and which are registered in
offshore locations. According to anti-corruption agency Transparency International, 44,022 properties in London are owned by
overseas companies, with nine out of ten of these being bought via

Construction and marketing suite in Nine Elms.

'secrecy jurisdictions' such as the British Virgin Islands, Jersey or the Isle of Man.[2] Some of the more notorious investors in London include Soulieman Marouf, an associate of Syrian President Bashar al-Assad; Alaa Mubarak, the son of former Egyptian President Hosni Mubarak; and Bukola Saraki, a Nigerian senator facing corruption charges, to name but a very few; Transparency International noted that 986 London properties are linked to 'politically exposed persons'. Marouf holds luxury flats in London worth almost £6 million, Mubarak is linked to a property worth £8 million in Knightsbridge and Sakari owns a property in Belgravia, with a second held by companies in which his wife and former special assistant are shareholders.[3]

Organized by the 'Committee for Legislation Against Moneylaundering in Properties by Kleptocrats', which calls itself ClampK, the Kleptocracy Tour took an assorted group of journalists and interested others on a journey around stratospherically expensive homes owned by billionaires from Russia and the former Soviet Union. With sponsorship by two American think tanks – the Hudson Institute and the Henry Jackson Society – the tour had a whiff of the new Cold War about it, but there was no arguing with the scale of Russian capital from dubious sources flowing straight into London property. We began with Whitehall Court, the former headquarters of MI6, which is now owned by the wife of a Russian minister. The tour bus then wended its way past Belgrave Square in Kensington, where a business tycoon, formerly the richest man in Russia, owned number 5, while oligarch Boris Berezovsky, who died in 2013, had several flats at number 26. At One Hyde Park in Knightsbridge one of Ukraine's richest men spent more than $197 million on two apartments. Although the focus was on Russians, we also took in 28 Wilton Place in Belgravia, owned by the son of a deposed African leader, which was covered in scaffolding and appeared to be undergoing renovations, leading to suspicions that they were back in town. Dr Ala'a Shehabi, a Bahraini pro-democracy activist and one of the founders of Bahrain Watch, took the mic and told the group that 'modern corruption today isn't about "the other", corruption has a white face and it's enabled by a network earning great fees'.

Next up was Brompton Road Tube station, closed in 1934, which was described by Borisovich as a 'third-grade nuclear bunker here in Central London'. It was bought in 2013 by Ukrainian oligarch Dmytro Firtash for £53 million, just days before he was arrested in Vienna at the FBI's request on suspicion of corruption and forming a criminal organization – charges he claims are politically motivated.[4]

From West London, the bus made its way to the West End and the traditional home of medical practice, Harley Street, which now combines discreet addresses for offshore companies with private doctors. At number 29 we were told that a paper trail from the Ukrainian presidential hunting lodge links to this front address. Then it was north to the exclusive enclaves of St John's Wood, where the bus briefly stopped outside 15 Acacia Road, bought by an offshore company for £23.25 million, although from the outside the modern red-brick home was striking only for just how bland and suburban it seemed. But if Acacia Road was markedly unexceptional, Witanhurst in Highgate was just the opposite. With its twenty-eight bedrooms, 40,000 square-foot basement and designer orangery, it is London's largest private house. 'It's a refuge, a showroom and deposit box,' Borisovich said of the palatial address, owned by a Russian tycoon who until recently served in Putin's senate.[5]

As the oligarchs move in, they are clashing with the retired liberal intellectuals of the Highgate Literary Society, who live in Lubetkin's modernist masterpiece Highpoint and are fighting the super-rich over contentious planning applications to tear down and rebuild homes. This old well-heeled elite never imagined that the great houses along the Hampstead–Highgate Ridge – which includes Kenwood House, which was gifted to the nation – would ever be owned by private individuals again. Now both Witanhurst and the other great house, Beechwood, are in oligarch hands. Academics Roger Burrows and Richard Webber researched the conflict between the heritage-minded old elite and the oligarchs' desires to build vast subterranean basements or demolish old properties altogether. They draw a parallel with pre-First World War levels of inequality which characterized the Edwardian era and highlight the similarity between the sources of wealth of the old industrialists – the first owner of

Witanhurst, in 1913, was English soap magnate Arthur Crosfield – and those of today's massive personal enrichment: oil, coal, telecoms and steel. The difference is that today's wealth is not created within national borders and the often absent owners of the big houses have little engagement with the local community, who encounter them only through the lawyers representing their planning applications. By the end of the day I felt tired and disorientated by this unusual city tour and the fantastical amount of money ploughed into these anonymous palatial properties.

Russian billionaires are far from the only ones who see London as a 'safe haven' for their money, and global instability simply fuels prices, a fact which the property industry is well aware of. When it comes to money laundering, an estate agent working in Kensington told me: 'We all know there was a period when anything goes. It's only recently that agents and solicitors have started asking questions, but often we're still not sure of the provenance of the party.'[6] The way properties are bought and sold, through intermediaries such as search agents and runners who look for properties on behalf of the super-rich, is often down to logistics such as buyers and their inner circle not speaking the language. But it also contributes to the anonymity of owners, facilitated by the lack of direct communication with estate agents, who are required to exercise a level of regulatory oversight through the UK Money Laundering Regulations 2007. Instead, tiers of middlemen create a shroud of secrecy that has come to characterize the top end of the market. According to a report which researched fourteen new landmark developments, 40 per cent of those homes have been sold to investors from high-corruption risk countries or those hiding behind anonymous companies.[7]

As to the relationship between foreign wars and London property, there is more than a tacit admission in the industry that one feeds the other, with one property executive commenting with brute honesty that 'every mortar bomb in Libya adds £1/sq foot to investments here'.[8] As the *Evening Standard* put it:

> If someone wanted to map the world's economic and political hotspots without watching the news, they could do a lot worse than

track London's property market. First the richest tycoons of Europe's sick economies plunged their cash into pads in Mayfair, Knightsbridge and Kensington to escape the eurozone debt crisis. Then the Arab Spring saw an influx of money from Middle Eastern tycoons. Next came the Russians and Ukrainians looking for a safe haven, and now the French and American super-rich are rushing into the capital to escape Hollande's and Obama's tax hikes.[9]

Following the election of Donald Trump as president of the United States, property investment company London Central Portfolio cheerily sent out an email to subscribers reflecting on the 'unprecedented turn of events', and pointing out that while

> the London property market will clearly not be top of your agenda today . . . it is London Central Portfolio's view that there will be a net positive impact on the market . . . as uncertainty on the political and economic state is heightened once again . . . Whilst all of this plays out, Prime Central London property, a traditional safe haven, is expected to benefit.[10]

'EXCHANGE VALUE'

> I know a lot of people that have second homes in London and I'm so glad they do. Even if they're here only for a few weeks and throw some key parties, these are amazing multiplying events.
>
> Patrik Schumacher, director of Zaha Hadid Architects

There is an argument that the concentration of billionaires and multimillionaires in a few limited areas has little impact on the lives and housing needs of most Londoners. Indeed, bringing wealth into the city is no bad thing, providing jobs and services and stimulating certain parts of the economy.

Rather than acknowledging the inflationary impact of global capital on London rents and house prices, the housing crisis is framed simply as a matter of supply and demand, with the super prime sector an issue of concern only to those interested in global finance, Londoners benefiting overall even while houses and buildings transfer to owners who view them as vehicles for investment rather than homes. This is the line ped- dled by Conservative politicians and many from other parties, who would have us believe that if we just build more homes prices will come down. But that is to miss the point, which is that the hugely inflated value of land in London is a direct result of the glut of foreign investment in the more expensive parts of the city, to an extent that it could be termed a 'super prime crisis'. The sub-prime crisis in the US, which trig- gered the 2008 financial crash, saw the frenzied trading of credit default swaps and collateralized debt obligations in very high-risk mortgages entirely break the connection with the reality of people on the ground, who were in no position to afford mortgages. Today, what economists call the 'exchange value' of housing in London, and many other parts of the UK, has entirely broken the connection with its 'use value'. Exchange value is the price of a commodity sold on the market, while its use value refers to its usefulness for people. When it comes to housing, prices are failing to respond to the needs of most people, allowing the influx of global capital, often from highly dubious sources, to utterly distort the market. The resulting crisis in affordability is affecting all layers of soci- ety. But the prevailing discussion around the housing crisis misses this story, claiming instead that attracting wealth is purely positive, bringing jobs and economic stimulus. The first task is to show how intercon- nected the super prime market is to the housing crisis in its entirety. It does create multiplying events, but not in fact positive ones. Rather, these multipliers displace people and create economic and social instability.

The way global capital distorts the housing market in London, with knock-on effects for the rest of the UK, happens through a pro- cess of 'trickle down', a phrase I'm borrowing from Margaret Thatcher, but with a different slant. For Thatcherites in the 1980s, trickle down was the justification for their economic revolution; the claim was that the great wealth generated by turning Britain into a financial centre would trickle down to the poorest people who needed it the most. This has manifestly failed to happen. It is the case that wealth does trickle down through places, but rather than benefiting the less well-off, it displaces them. This is true for every community in London from the old English elites who can no longer afford to live in Kensington and Chelsea to the residents of social housing forced out of their homes as estates are razed and luxury flats arise in their place.

Alison, a well-heeled older English woman who used to live in South Kensington, described how the process affected her family, forcing her son and his family to move out from central London to Acton, as he could no longer afford to live in Kensington where he had grown up.

'John grew up in Kensington, and he would really like to stay in Kensington, but there's no way they could have afforded the kind of house that they . . . well anything really because it's just ridiculous, the property prices,' she said.[11] Savills, the property company, identified this trend of displacement as far back as 2011. They put a much more positive spin on it, claiming it was a cause for celebration as it represented the spreading of wealth around the UK rather than the catalyst for unaffordable housing prices throughout the country.

> As many as one in five buyers in southwest London come directly out of central London, as equity funnelled in at the centre migrates down London's wealth corridors. So, as billionaires displace multi-millionaires from the top addresses, so they in their turn displace millionaires. Equity migrates to more peripheral areas of the capital and, eventually, out of the capital to the rest of the UK as homeowners invest their equity in country houses, second homes and retirement properties and so housing wealth and the prime effect spread,

wrote Savills.[12] This is the supposed positive effect of trickle down in property.

The process of speculation and displacement driving the super prime and prime markets in London is underpinned by foreign investment, which is not limited to oligarchs and is, like the rest of the housing market, characterized by a complex series of submarkets. According to data provider Experian these submarkets include categories such as Global Power Brokers, who reside in certain parts of London. The Experian guide describes how the names of the neighbourhoods that contain Global Power Brokers are hallmarks of exclusive London living – Mayfair, St James, Belgravia, Kensington, Chelsea, Notting Hill, Marylebone, St Johns Wood, Hampstead. They are clustered around Hyde and Regent Parks, and are the only areas that wealthy non-domiciled London residents would consider living in.[13]

The demand driving the housing market in these areas, and trickling down throughout the city and the rest of the country, is coming from a very particular market of what are known as 'High Net Worth Individuals' – of whom there are estimated to be in excess of 500,000 in the UK, mostly in London – and 'Ultra High Net Worth Individuals', who have in excess of $30 million, and billionaires. Academics call these super-rich groups 'transnational elites', whose wealth is invested internationally, who travel intensively and who have globally based social networks. Today they are clustered in the super prime parts of London, the world capital of billionaires, with seventy-seven, sixteen more than its nearest rival, New York.[14] These groups have seen their wealth increase significantly since the financial crisis, boosted by the policy of Quantitative Easing, introduced by the Bank of England in the UK, the Federal Reserve in the US and the European Central Bank, which pushed up asset prices, including stocks and shares, gilts and property prices. The Bank of England itself recognized that in the UK this policy increased the financial wealth held outside pension funds of the top 5 per cent of households, who now hold 40 per cent of assets.[15] This influx of capital has fuelled the property market since 2008. London property is now the most sought after in the world, according to property consultancy firm Knight Frank, beating New York for two years in a row to win the title of 'most important city to UHNWIs', with Singapore, Hong Kong, Shanghai and Dubai coming next. Knight Frank's survey of super-rich clients also asked what could change London's position, and respondents were clear that tax and regulation were top of the list, with changes to taxation in first place, followed by changes to financial regulation. Terrorism was another factor which ranked as marginally more of a problem in New York than in London.[16]

THE MONACO GROUP

In Kensington and Chelsea, home to around 4,900 Ultra High Net Worth Individuals,[17] I had arranged to meet Daniel Moylan. Moylan was formerly deputy leader of the council and a past adviser to Boris Johnson and remains a councillor of twenty-seven years' standing. Walking down Kensington High Street on my way to meet him, I passed what used to be Ken Market, once a bohemian magnet for punks with their pink mohicans, who lolled about outside the indoor market when I was a child. The market catered to every subculture of music and fashion and was where Freddie Mercury had a stall before Queen became famous. In the 1980s, I was at school in nearby Hammersmith and used to hang out at the pool hall in the basement around the back, which was the place to be for teenagers from many different backgrounds from all over London. It is now a large PC World topped by mirrored glass office blocks.

We met at the Royal Garden Hotel, on the corner of Kensington Gardens. Always a wealthy place, Kensington used to be, like many affluent parts of London, a mixed and diverse neighbourhood, home to people from different income brackets and backgrounds. Over coffee, Moylan agreed that the area has changed but didn't see it as direct displacement. 'I am aware that the older generation of English upper-class money has tended to die off and be replaced by a different set of buyers. Is it regrettable? You can have a certain nostalgia about it but you have to see what you're having nostalgia about – a class-based sense of entitlement.' He argues that 'being open to all sorts of people, including the super-rich, does something to the character of a city that has positive elements', contrasting London to mega cities such as São Paolo or Bangkok, which he claims do not compete in 'global city' rankings because they are not first-choice locations for 'alpha elites'. I thought this comparison with such cities painted a possible future vision of London.

Later, as we walked around the Georgian squares and terraces in the back streets of Kensington, the quiet was punctuated by the drilling of new so-called 'iceberg' basements which, as in Highgate and other alpha parts of London, are a signifier of the super-rich, and can apparently cost in the region of £3 million apiece. Two to three to a street, the basements have become a flash point of conflict between old and new money with existing and often elderly residents fighting vicious planning battles against the constant disruption. In one particularly bizarre case, Kensington resident and property developer Zipporah Lisle-Mainwaring painted her multi-million pound townhouse in red and white stripes in protest after the council rejected her application to build a two-storey basement. While it's difficult to get accurate figures, it's clear the rejection of Lisle-Mainwaring's application goes against the trend; 450 basements were granted planning permission in the borough in 2013,[18] with the figure likely to be much higher today. Walking past the stripy house, Moylan pointed out another large home, previously owned by an admiral who died in his nineties, and which had been bought by an international banker. 'The first thing he did was put in a planning application for a swimming pool in the basement – it's a small illustration of how it happens,' he told me. Another consequence he described of the changing demographics of the area is that, alongside the incomers, original residents are 'clinging on in the face of total impoverishment'. The result is that asset-rich but cash-poor older people sit in multi-million pound houses unable to turn the heating on because they can't afford to. It was upsetting to think of frail, elderly people freezing in their homes because they didn't want to move.

London's relatively lax tax laws for foreign corporations and individuals and its strong links with offshore dependencies have led to claims that the capital is now the biggest tax haven in the world. In his book *Treasure Islands*, Nicholas Shaxson describes London as the centre of a spider's web that links to the Channel Islands, the Isle of Man and the Caribbean.[19] This impression of super prime London as a tax haven to rival Monaco is borne out by the everyday experience of residents. Helen Kirwan-Taylor, a journalist who writes for the *Sunday Times*, lives on one of the most prestigious roads in

Notting Hill. She moved in twenty-two years ago as part of an earlier wave of 'super gentrification'[20] characterized by the arrival of very wealthy professionals working in the City of London. 'We were the generation of bankers who pushed out the artists and journalists – our home was lived in by two elderly artists, there was a film reviewer next door,' she remembered. 'The bankers pushed out the artists, then the next wave came – this neighbourhood has become Monaco.' Today it's mostly made up of 'super-wealthy connected European families with trust funds so complicated you need a PhD to work it out. They're all too young to be making this much money – when you've got young children and you're buying a house for £22 million you're not making that. They're complicated tax exiles – I suspect a lot of them are non doms.'

'There are a couple of tell-tale signs you're in Monaco. Houses have not one, but two Filipinos – if not three,' she said, describing the trend among the super-rich to hire domestic staff from the Phillippines. The upshot is that 'all the services around here are now dealing with the Monaco group. I called the chiropodist to ask how much they charge and they said £150 – I almost dropped the phone.' Alongside tax, the other key factor that attracts the Monaco group is the schools, an interplay between property prices and schools which characterizes the whole city. On her road her neighbours include an Icelandic billionaire, an Australian who lives in New York part time, a Turkish/Dutch family and a Norwegian/Israeli family, a set of nationalities that reflects the global nature of the transnational wealth which is coming into the city. London is seen as safe, both in terms of physical safety and as a financial safe haven, and as well as appropriate schooling it has high-end restaurants and the right types of social life. Isabel, who described herself as a 'socialite', told researchers investigating the alpha elites that it was this mix that made it so appealing to Russians. 'So London is considered to be, well, just the place to go for a parallel life where your family is safe and everything is fine [. . .] London is easy. They've got the infrastructure, they've got everything, they're catered for, they have the Russian art events, they have the Sotheby's arts week with Russian art, they basically don't need to – adapt . . . You have the business run in Russia but live here – it's very often that business is in Russia and they have their family here and they fly over, they commute from Moscow on a weekly basis. So Sunday nights and BA flights, Heathrow, Moscow.'[21]

What impact does it have on community when 25 per cent of residential properties in Knightsbridge and Belgravia are empty most of the time, rising to 40 per cent in the West End?[22] The overlapping series of submarkets at the alpha end of the housing market have spawned a whole range of phrases to describe them, from 'buy to live' and 'buy to let', to 'buy for the children' and 'buy to leave'. Now investors purchase properties and don't even consider it necessary to rent them out: first and foremost the increase in property value is what they are after. The consequence is that the most exclusive parts of the city are almost entirely deserted and shrouded in darkness by evening, a trend which is equally coming to define parts of Manhattan.[23] Among these are properties which may be used only for a few weeks or months of the year, as the new elites replicate the British elite of old and come to London for their version of 'the season'.[24]

This leads to other tensions. Part of the summer season for some super-rich young men involves importing their Ferraris and Lamborghinis, the sound of screaming engines and screeching tyres reverberating around Sloane Square and Knightsbridge. The council has put in place a new kind of 'supercar ASBO' to combat 'anti-social driving', including revving engines, repeated acceleration, performing stunts and racing,[25] after complaints from thousands of residents. The 'Rich Kids of London' Instagram account documents other lifestyle excesses and was the subject of an awestruck *Evening Standard* profile of Luthra, one of the 21-year-old stars of the account, whose father owns clothing factories in India. Asked why he liked London, Luthra said: 'London's got everything you want. Culture? Check. Clubs? Check. And everything else is just forty-five minutes by plane. I can be in Monaco for the night or I can go to Paris for dinner.' The previous night he had been at Mahiki until 6 a.m., which he said was 'a £20K night', the following night he would be at nightclub DSTRKT and the day after that he would enter a super car rally in Ibiza.[26]

So what is the link between the housing crisis of the majority and the boy racers, the 'stateless MBA beings'* and the tax exiles who don't have to work because their property portolio earns far more than they ever could? The super prime market displaces established communities to new areas, driving up property and rent prices elsewhere. And as current policies are geared to attracting foreign investment and building luxury apartments rather than affordable homes, there is nothing to act as a counterweight. Once unfashionable zone 3, places like Acton in West London, Turnpike Lane and South Tottenham in North London, West Norwood in South London and Forest Gate in East London, become property hotspots, affecting the local community. Even Catford, described by long-term resident and *Guardian* columnist Lucy Mangan as 'the only place in all of London and the south-east to remain impervious to gentrification', is starting to see the usual suspects springing up – hipster cafés, delis and a vintage-style tea room.

The changes in all these places will be pleasant for many new residents and existing ones lucky enough to already own their homes – who will mostly be pushing fifty and above – but they will add further pressure to property prices and rents. The middle-class couple therefore unable to start a family in London might move to Bristol, Folkestone or Hastings, bringing similar patterns of property price speculation and displacement to these towns and cities. But it also impacts private tenants on housing benefit, who get pushed into shocking conditions in temporary accommodation, perhaps even as far out as Margate, which is becoming an unusual mix of priced-out London artists and creatives alongside a large homeless population in temporary accommodation. So from Kensington to Acton, from Acton to Forest Gate and from Forest Gate to the South Coast, individuals, couples and families – both the middle classes and the so-called 'claimant cultures' and working poor – are pushed out of London altogether. This is the 'super prime crisis', and it affects everyone. Very large injections of global capital into London's safe haven, including corrupt money, have combined with quantitative easing,

* Quote by Helen Kirwan-Taylor, referring to the transnational finance professionals with business degrees

limited regulation, flexible employment and some of the lowest corporate tax rates in the world, to transform London in under a decade.

INSIDE AND OUTSIDE THE TENT

The properties in the alpha parts of the city are in old and established areas of London, but the tens of thousands of luxury apartments in newly created districts are an equally important component of the housing crisis. The majority are sold 'off plan' – sold from plans before they are built – to overseas investors before they are marketed to Londoners. At Silvertown in the Royal Docks, by the Emirates Airline cable car, a proposed 'new piece of city' of thousands of balcony apartments, aimed at foreign investors renting out properties to the Canary Wharf workforce, is taking shape. A local resident told me she thinks most properties are sold and resold several times abroad before even hitting local estate agents. Silvertown is part of Newham Council's 'Arc of Opportunity', which is portrayed by the council as 'a regeneration supernova' in a promotional film made by Newham for Shanghai's world trade fair, the Shanghai Expo. The film airbrushes existing residents out of the picture almost entirely, except as participants of a generic 'street market' scene, interspersing images of London icons such as red telephone boxes with captions reminding viewers that it is 'just six hours from New York' and 'three hours from Paris', hitting all the right buttons for Asian and Chinese investors, who may know little about London, let alone Silvertown.

Property in London – and cities such as Manchester, Liverpool or Birmingham – is predicted to be a fast-expanding market for Chinese investors, in particular with Brexit and falls in the value of the pound. 'Our thesis – and this is supported by quite a lot of evidence – is that in many ways the international Chinese investment journey is probably just starting,' said Charles Pittar, chief executive of Juwai.com, a website that pairs buyers from the Chinese mainland with property developers. 'It's a big market now, but it is likely to be anywhere from two to four times the size in ten years' time,' he said, highlighting that, while all the headlines are about globetrotting tycoons, in China demand from the middle class is likely to be a key factor, driven by four main motivations: investment, lifestyle, emigration and education for their children.[27] So this pressure on London's housing – as a locus for global investment, pushing out local investment due to a lack of controls – doesn't appear to be going anywhere. This only increases the need for proper scrutiny of the full picture of the crisis.

International expos and property fairs are the meat and drink of this property industry. I managed to inveigle my way into the London Real Estate Forum, which is one of the property networking events of the year and a perfect illustration of how deals between developers, investors and local authorities are done. Organized by New London Architecture, a membership organization for developers, architects and other related bodies, it takes place every year in a giant marquee in Berkeley Square in Mayfair, at the heart of super prime London. I entered the marquee and saw a bar with a pyramid of filled champagne glasses at one end, while waitresses, immaculately clad in black cocktail dresses and heels, handed out sushi to delegates who milled around exhibition stands belonging to the likes of Southwark, Lambeth, Haringey, Croydon and Newham councils, who were advertising their wares in a slick and sophisticated marketing atmosphere light years away from the traditional image of the unglamorous local authority. Councils, working in partnership with developers, identify and earmark parts of the city for large-scale schemes and then tout them to the audience of global investors. As I walked around I saw a local authority head of regeneration I knew and asked her why she was there, taking two days out of her busy schedule for the event. 'The reason we come is because everybody's here. If I talk to five investors today then it's job done. Then we can choose who we work with,' she explained.

According to the website the event brings together more than 2,000 foreign investors, property companies, local authorities and politicians, as well as armies of consultants and PR people. Alongside the two-day networking event, a dizzying array of panel discussions and 'development showcases' in specially erected conference rooms provided a PR opportunity for developers and local authorities to pitch to investors and to each other; the 180-acre development planned for Brent Cross in North London, the fifteen developments and new town centre at Elephant and Castle in South London, the Earls Court development in West London and an unprecedented twenty-eight sites in Newham in East London were just a handful of the 180 showcases featured. It seemed as if every inch of the capital was being parcelled up and recreated in CGI images.

At the Southwark stand Neil Kirby, head of regeneration for the south of the borough, told a small audience about Southwark's latest plans: 'Old Kent Road is the newest regeneration area, in the context of the Bakerloo Line being extended. We're expecting planning applications for 4,000 homes in the next year. Landowners are coming to us at the rate of two a day at the moment.' Deirdra Armsby, director of regeneration and planning at Newham, described to delegates the astonishing number of sites in her borough ripe for development. 'We have the huge benefit in our borough of a young and accepting population ready to accept this scale of growth. One of these sites would be unusual – we have twenty-eight strategic sites in our planning policy framework.' The huge opposition to plans by Newham to demolish the Carpenters Estate and the subsequent high-profile occupation of a flat on the estate by campaign group Focus E15 led to University College London pulling out of its joint venture to build a new campus on the site and challenges Armsby's account of Newham's 'accepting population'. But at this particular gathering the only note of dissent came from Councillor Ken Clark, who said somewhat bashfully: 'It is magnificent what we're doing in East London and I'm honoured to play a role as the cabinet member for regeneration but there is the question of affordability – I know that's a bit of a social issue to raise in this environment.' His comment, which was not followed up by anyone in the room, was the only attempt made to link the tsunami of investment and regeneration with the housing affordability crisis.

Sitting down at lunchtime for sandwiches of rare roast beef on sourdough and smoked salmon on rye, I asked the woman next to me why she was there. 'We've come from Singapore because we want to invest. Everyone wants to invest in London.' Across the table, a young man approached a group having a meeting. 'I just wanted to say hello and introduce myself. I'm an investor, what are you up to?' he asked. 'Oh, we're just freeloaders,' the more senior in the group replied laughing, before adding, 'We have developments – our objective here is to meet politicians and local authorities.' It was quite an eye-opener into the frenzied extent of networking, which is undeniably useful for all the key protagonists. The problem is one of accountability and transparency, with all the deal making taking place behind closed doors; when I asked for a delegate list I was told there wasn't one, and when I followed this up with New London Architecture I was told it wasn't in a shareable format. They promised they would send me a list in due course, but I never heard any more about it.

As lunch went on, it became very noisy, as the sound of klaxons, chants and a megaphone outside became impossible to ignore, although almost everyone blithely tried to. I walked out of the marquee and into a wall of noise in Berkeley Square – whistles, police sirens and chants. 'Here are the people responsible for the housing crisis. Here are the people selling off our land. There are eighteen councils here, fifteen of them are Labour,' a man shouted into a loudhailer. 'Tell your friends in Hong Kong and China this is what will happen when they invest in London property.' It was Simon Elmer, from Architects for Social Housing, along with housing campaigners I knew from the Aylesbury Estate in South London, which is under threat of demolition. Aysen Denis, who lives on the Aylesbury and is fighting to save her home, came up to me and said: 'Sorry I haven't been in touch. I've just wanted to hide recently.' As I walked out past the security guards, the protest was intimidating, and when one of the protesters recognized me she apologized for shouting at me. Once amid the throng of protesters, I saw it wasn't threatening, and the noise of the police siren turned out to be more of a joke – activated by a button on the loudhailer. But for most of the delegates it was surely discomfiting. One woman in a smart royal blue dress pushed one of the protesters and was hissed and booed as she walked down the ramp to the marquee, before starting to run and falling over. Mostly the well-dressed men (and it was nearly all men) just laughed but in the most unpleasant incident a delegate called a protester a 'poof'.

Outside the tent the demonstration exposed the lack of democratic oversight of the regeneration process, as communities from many estates facing demolition protested that they had been stripped of any say in their future. But inside, amid the relentlessly upbeat PR atmosphere, there was no discussion of the wider consequences of foreign investment and regeneration and the impact they have on affordability and communities.

The property industry has long worked on the basis of deals struck between individuals, oiled by personal connections and good relationships. MIPIM* is the grandfather of these property fairs, which include exhibition areas, networking events and conference sessions. It is no coincidence that it began in 1990 as Reaganomics and the trickle-down ideology embedded themselves on both sides of the Atlantic and the global property industry began to take off. Rumour has it that more champagne is consumed at MIPIM than during the Cannes Film Festival, and during the 1990s and 2000s it came to be seen as an essential part of the property calendar, with the canapé receptions on the yachts along the Croisette, a not to be missed jolly for the emerging alliance of developers, PRs, investors, politicians and local authorities. One anecdote has former London Mayor Ken Livingstone apologizing for arriving late for a meeting because he'd spent too long in the jacuzzi.[28]

Since 2014, when the MIPIM franchise launched MIPIM UK in London, every significant property industry event in London has been accompanied by protests about the housing crisis, with campaign groups such as Architects for Social Housing claiming that developers, investors and local authorities are demolishing council estates and building luxury apartments in their place. At MIPIM London in 2015, conference sessions included: 'London – from social housing to super prime' and 'The Downing Street Forum',[29] which

---

* *Marché international des professionels de l'immobilier* (international market of real estate professionals)

offered investors and developers direct access to leading political figures. Outside, Architects for Social Housing gave free consultations to housing protesters and campaigners for council estates threatened with demolition, while Streets Kitchen provided food for homeless and hungry people. After I left the protest I'd witnessed, I went back into the high-security enclosure of the Real Estate Forum and slipped into another conference session. As I sat down the heavens opened and an alarming monsoon-like thunderstorm started hammering down on the roof of the marquee. 'It's gone a bit quiet on the protester front,' the first speaker said, to appreciative laughter from the audience, invoking a level of real hostility which seemed to reflect accurately the 'Class War' banner of the protesters outside.

LUXURY APARTMENT LAND

If property fairs like the London Real Estate Forum and MIPIM are all about schmoozing and deal making, I also wanted to know what the places the deals create are really like. Building a 'new piece of city' is a slow process which takes years and rarely emerges on the gargantuan scale promised by breathless press releases. Not all the 180 gleaming new districts in the forum's brochures and showcases will see the light of day and, even if they do, they are unlikely to be built in their entirety. That said, London is everywhere characterized by cranes and construction with parts of the city, such as Elephant and Castle and Vauxhall Nine Elms, changing beyond all recognition.

One of the most epic developments, both in terms of its size and its iconic status, is Vauxhall Nine Elms, going up around Battersea Power Station and the new American embassy. The power station, subject to numerous failed attempts to redevelop it since it closed in 1983, is a post-industrial opportunity for the capital bar none, in a part of the city long characterized by light industry, arterial roads and poor public transport. A cultural landmark of historical significance, the power station was designed by Sir Giles Gilbert Scott, designer of Bankside Power Station (now Tate Modern), Waterloo Bridge and the classic red telephone box. It is a Grade II listed building with a lavish art deco interior, but instead of being opened up to the city, it is destined to be a high-class gated community, like every single one of the countless other new quarters planned for London.

My first glimpse, from the window of an overground train, of the new Battersea Power Station development was the gold cladding of one of the apartment blocks which in its ostentation brought to mind Damien Hirst's diamond-encrusted skull, sold for £50 million in 2007, just before the financial crisis. Keen to have a proper look at the place, I took the bus from Sloane Square across Chelsea Bridge to the power station, which is still hard to get to and will remain so until the Northern Line extension opens in 2020. From Chelsea Bridge clusters of towers of brand-new balconied apartments mushroom one behind the other as far as the eye can see, in developments with names like Vista, Chelsea Bridge. Access to the 42-acre construction site was about a mile away down Battersea Park Road, now defined by a hoarding stretching its length and low-rise council housing on the other side of the busy road. I passed a well-designed 1930s-style poster pointing the way to the Frank Gehry Show Apartment and rounded the corner to see a security gate and sentry box. Unlike high street estate agents, where interested purchasers can just walk in, visits to the Experience Suites of forthcoming developments are mainly by appointment. This was confirmed to me by the security guard who explained I would need to contact the sales team in advance and that 'you need to be interested in buying a flat'. I don't really go in for undercover journalism but needs must, so I said I was looking at properties for my boss who lived abroad and I managed to blag my way in.

There are seven phases planned for the development, of which three were under construction at the time of writing. Phase 1 is at Circus West, with the first residents moving in during 2017; it was apparently already sold off plan before it was built, although that didn't necessarily mean properties were unavailable to purchase. For off plan sales, as the sales manager explained to me, buyers put down a £5,000 reservation fee, followed by 10 per cent of the price the following year, 10 per cent in the third year and the balance on completion. In a rising market this amounts to a tidy profit on resale values, for investors who have no intention of ever actually buying or going near the development. Although she said Phase 1 was sold, I got the strong impression from the sales manager that if I had expressed a serious interest in buying there, chances are I would have been able to, meaning that they were effectively paving the way for the resale of properties which were already sold. The speculative gains to be made from off plan sales in a rising market also mean that, should the property market collapse, off plan sales are unlikely to translate into actual sales, creating structural instability in the market from the outset.

The second phase is the restoration of the power station itself, which will feature a 2,000-seater venue on the second floor and a Norman Foster-designed infinity pool on the roof, while Phase 3 will see the creation of Electric Boulevard, a new high street connecting the development with the Northern Line extension, flanked by apartments designed by Frank Gehry and Norman Foster. The architecture critic and writer Rowan Moore described the scheme as 'so richly fed on world class architecture' that it 'has managed a feat that might have been thought impossible, which was to make the power station look small'.[30] Inside the Frank Gehry show home the open plan 'LA style' apartment was very pleasant, with its 'winter garden' balcony and architect-designed interiors, although the ceilings seemed low. For £1.7 million for a two-bedroom flat, pleasant is perhaps the least one might expect.

The Battersea Power Station Development Company is selling not just iconic living, but trying to offer the ultimate contemporary lifestyle experience. The gold cladding, private members' club and rooftop pool give a decadent feel to the development, which has been seen by some as a potential symbol of the market overreaching itself. *The Placebook*, an extraordinary coffee table book of unusually lavish promotional material, details how a 'place director' will be employed who 'will have a master's degree in authenticity', and who will eschew corporate chains and Disneyfication and 'do everything possible to avoid the obvious', enabling the company to create 'the final climax community'. This will be nurtured by 'those special early individuals, with a hunger for newness and an eye for the next big thing' in the shape of quirky independent shops – in this case a luxury florist, upmarket butcher and artisan baker – that will sit alongside luxury brands. A lot of effort is going into this attempt to create what the sales manager described to me as a place which is 'self-sufficient – almost a city within a city'. There will also be a new riverside park and public square, although the high street, new 'public' square and park will all be privately owned and privately controlled, with restrictions on public access and behaviour, a visible high-security presence in the shape of uniformed security guards and blanket CCTV coverage. The imprimatur of the Malaysian consortium that owns the development, which includes the largest developer in Malaysia, SP Setia, and a Malaysian sovereign wealth fund, is reflected by the naming of the new square as Malaysia Square; this echoes Canada Square in Canary Wharf, named for its Canadian investors twenty-five years ago, when this model of private ownership and control of large parts of the city really began in the UK. For the last fifteen years it has been the template for all new development and means that every 'new piece of city' is privately owned and removed from a democratically accountable, genuinely public realm.

Down the road from the power station, although quite different in terms of branding and lifestyle, is Embassy Gardens, London's new diplomatic quarter and the home of the US and Dutch embassies. Only the first phase was complete – and looked strangely unprepossessing – as I approached a block of brick-built flats above a Waitrose. The Experience Suite offered more trappings of luxury, although the show flats seemed rather small, an effect surely enhanced by the heavyweight furniture and red velvet and gilt furnishings, presumably deemed appropriate for diplomats. The best value seemed to be a one-room studio cleverly divided by a glass partition, for £635,000, but the relative affordability of this tiny one-room space was only in comparison with everything else I had seen. The jewel in the crown of Embassy Gardens is the Sky Pool, which is a swimming pool suspended ten storeys in the air, spanning the space between two tower blocks. Part of The Orangery, a private members' club for residents and their friends, the Sky Pool has been seen as a symbol of the divisive housing market, with the super-rich literally able to look down on everyone else while they swim. As none of these attractions were yet complete the helpful agent I spoke to suggested that to get a feel for the place, I go into the lobby of one of the completed buildings, which boasted lots of marble, three security guards and pseudo-libraries with shelves of books and sofas where visitors can wait. A slightly forlorn sign announced that *Ghostbusters* was playing in the private cinema and Tony Blair's autobiography sat on one of the coffee tables.

Because of the time I've spent in Elephant and Castle I was also keen to visit the Elephant Park Experience Suite, which is on the ground floor of One The Elephant, a luxury development by developer Lendlease in the centre of twenty proposed new towers in Elephant and Castle. In this case, the show flat was a pristine two-bedroom apartment, notable for being a lot smaller than those I had visited on the Heygate and Aylesbury estates, with small rooms and low ceilings – at 2.5 metres, the minimum advisable height according to the Mayor's Design Guide. But what was particularly strange was that, unlike in the other show homes, there were no real windows. Instead I found myself surrounded by fake windows and a fake balcony with fake views painted on, of places that didn't yet exist. The unreality of the experience reminded me of the last exhibition stand I visited before leaving the London Real Estate Forum, which was Deloitte Digital, the digital innovation arm of the global consultancy. Two young and enthusiastic techie guys were offering interested passers-by the chance to experience a CGI fly-through of apartments in a proposed new development. I put on a pair of virtual reality goggles and queasily lurched through an apartment in a tower block surrounded by a view of a Manhattan-style cityscape, feeling as if I was in a version of a video game. Deloitte Digital were marketing their product at the forum because this is a tool which is already being used to sell properties and which potential purchasers from all over the world can interact with to suggest changes they would like to see. The show homes of apartments not yet built, which might never be built, and the digital fly-throughs of virtual reality apartments and cityscapes which don't exist were for me the ultimate symbol of just how decoupled from reality the property market has become.

2
The Financialization of
Housing and Planning

THE POSTWAR HOUSING SETTLEMENT

How did we get to this point, where house prices and rents are unaffordable for the majority? In 1948, Aneurin Bevan, minister for health in the postwar Labour government, famously founded the National Health Service, which was based on the principle that it would be free at the point of use. Despite ongoing battles over privatization, this has remained the cornerstone of the NHS ever since. Less well known is the fact that Bevan's remit also covered housing and that just a year later he introduced the Housing Act of 1949, which removed the restriction on public housing as being only for the working class, paving the way for his idea of modern mixed communities. At the time he said: 'We should try to introduce in our modern villages and towns what was always the lovely feature of English and Welsh villages, where the doctor, the grocer, the butcher and the farm labourer all lived in the same street. I believe that it is essential for the full life of citizens . . . to see the living tapestry of a mixed community.'

In the 1950s and 60s Conservative and Labour governments competed with each other to see who could build the most public housing, which was an absolute necessity following the massive bomb damage to Britain's towns and cities during the Second World War. There was also a desire to improve conditions in the inner cities by replacing slums with high rises of 'streets in the sky' with indoor toilets and hot running water. Partly as a result of problems associated with mass system building, the process provoked much controversy, particularly

Part of new Lendlease development Elephant Park,
adjacent to a cleared site from the demolished Heygate Estate.

over the displacement of existing communities as slums were cleared. But while mistakes were made, between 1945 and 1980 hundreds of thousands of homes were built every year, approximately a third by councils and two thirds by the private sector, with councils building nearly half of all housing in bumper years. This was paralleled by a similar emphasis on public house building in many other European countries and even in the US. Postwar, the West, with an eye to the housing and healthcare provision beyond the Iron Curtain, made great efforts to harness the benefits of economic growth to improved living standards to show that capitalist societies could also provide public goods. In 1978, the last year before Margaret Thatcher came to power, the government built 100,000 council homes and the private sector built 150,000. There was no shortage of housing. Since 1979, while private sector house building figures have remained about the same, the government builds hardly any. Housing associations were meant to pick up the shortfall, but build about a tenth of the numbers required. The graph overleaf of the homes built in the postwar period provides the clearest possible visual illustration of just how much impact the failure to build public housing has had.

Today, Bevan's vision of the doctor, the grocer and the labourer living in the same street seems filtered through rose-tinted spectacles, but it isn't a million miles away from the Britain I grew up in. When I was a child in London in the 1970s, and even into the 1980s, council housing did provide homes for a wide range of people, more than a third of whom were on above-average incomes. I didn't live in council housing but some of my friends did – which is not surprising given that in 1981 a third of *all* Londoners lived in council housing. And their houses weren't so different from mine. I 'played out' and rollerskated around estates, which were hardly alien places. They were no socialist utopia either, but life for many people on council estates was OK and certainly much better than the fight for survival that it is today, with many tenants at the sharp end of austerity policies and fighting campaigns to save their estates from demolition.

During the 1980s, council estates began to change. The impact of Margaret Thatcher's flagship Right to Buy policy that saw the sell-off

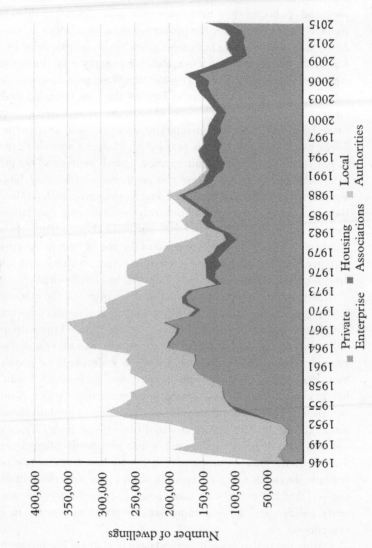

Permanent dwellings completed in England by tenure, 1946 to 2015

Number of dwellings

400,000
350,000
300,000
250,000
200,000
150,000
100,000
50,000

1946 1949 1952 1955 1958 1961 1964 1967 1970 1973 1976 1979 1982 1985 1988 1991 1994 1997 2000 2003 2006 2009 2012 2015

■ Private Enterprise ■ Housing Associations ■ Local Authorities

of millions of council homes at very large discounts, which began in the 1980s and continues to this day, is well known and cannot be underestimated. Even at the time the BBC reported: 'The government believes the bill will transform the social structure of Britain for good,'[1] which it did, but perhaps not in the way that was intended. The BBC report went on to quote Shelter which predicted the outcome would be housing shortages and homelessness, closer to what we see now. Right to Buy was justifiably popular because it transferred wealth to the less well-off. But the key point about the policy was that councils were forbidden from using the revenue raised from the sale of council homes to build new ones. As the emphasis moved away from building new subsidized council housing, it shifted towards subsidizing housing for people on lower incomes through housing benefit, which was introduced in 1982. This change from subsidizing the *supply* of new homes to subsidizing the *demand* for housing underpins housing policy today. It is behind the enormous escalation in the housing benefit bill, expected to be £24 billion in 2017,[2] and is responsible for the dysfunctional market in housing the poor through the private rented sector. Social housing is no longer celebrated, nor is it seen as a part of what a good government should supply to its people.

The starkest symbol of the journey we have travelled from Bevan's postwar vision of mixed communities to the financialization of housing was symbolized by the opening ceremony of the 2014 Commonwealth Games in Glasgow, when the city council decided to broadcast the demolition of the Red Road flats 'live' to an audience of billions around the world. The resulting outcry saw Glaswegians 'immobilized in disbelief',[3] while former Member of the Scottish Parliament Carolyn Leckie launched a petition against the plans which gathered thousands of signatures. 'What on earth were the people who decided this thinking of?' she questioned. 'Can you imagine if Danny Boyle's celebration of the NHS at the [London 2012] Olympics involved blowing up an NHS hospital?' Glasgow's politicians backtracked but the very fact that knocking down a housing estate was even considered appropriate for a worldwide celebration of Britain reflects a widespread view among the political class that the death of social housing, and with it the modernist ideal of good-quality housing for all, is a triumph to be celebrated.

THE POSTWAR PLANNING SETTLEMENT AND THE PUBLIC GOOD

If the price of food had increased at the same rate as house prices in the UK over the last forty years, then today a chicken would cost more than £50.[4] As average house prices in London are more than twice those in the rest of the country, if food prices had tracked house price inflation, in London that chicken would cost £100. High rates of inflation in the 1970s were among the factors that propelled Margaret Thatcher's Conservatives to power in 1979, and since then low inflation has been a source of economic pride for successive governments. But while food, clothes, furniture, cars and holidays are all included in the government's preferred inflation index, the Consumer Prices Index (CPI), house prices are not, nor are rents accurately reflected.* So inflation in UK housing, which has increased by 166 per cent since the 1970s and an eye-watering 513 per cent in London, compared, for example, with Germany, where it has been virtually stable, is treated differently from every other form of inflation because it has been stripped out of official records. The paradox, of course, is that housing is also a property asset – as well as a human right and public good – and rising prices benefit owners. The result in the UK is a situation where one part of the population is pitted against the other, with those who own gaining directly from the rising prices that exclude everyone else. Despite the mythology that we are a nation of homeowners Britain has rarely exceeded the European average and we have now plummeted to the fourth lowest home ownership in Europe, with only Denmark, Austria and Germany showing lower rates of owner occupation.[5] The

---

* Housing costs were partially included in the previous index, the Retail Price Index, but that was replaced by former Chancellor Gordon Brown in 2003, a change critics put down to house price inflation running at more than 20 per cent at the time.

difference is that these are all countries with a famously high-quality, affordable rental sector, where people want to rent rather than buy. Today, although the great majority of people in the UK would like to get on to the property ladder, home ownership is at the same level as it was in 1986, when Margaret Thatcher was just embarking on her housing revolution.

To an extent, this is part of the global trend that in the contemporary economy the rate of return on capital is greater than economic growth; rising prices mean that buying property is the best way for people to make money. For domestic investors, it makes sense to buy as much property as possible, which keeps prices high (although in London, and increasingly other cities such as Bristol and Manchester, the flood of global capital is the main driver for soaring inflation). At the same time as property prices have risen, wages have failed to keep pace, even among those on high incomes, resulting in more than a third of households being locked out of the housing market, with mortgages running at multiples of five times incomes (another factor that keeps prices high, as those who have managed to save for the substantial deposit required can then afford expensive homes). But while similar trends are evident in other parts of the world, in the UK the extent of our inflated house prices is down to the particular circumstance that we have very high land prices compared to other countries. This is the consequence of a malfunctioning planning system that no longer bears any relationship to what its architects intended. Like the housing settlement, the planning system was created as part of the postwar consensus to serve the public good, but since the mid-1980s it has been distorted out of all recognition and no longer works, becoming instead a mechanism for fuelling speculation.

Shortly before Bevan paved the way for mass council house building with the Housing Act 1949, the Town and Country Planning Act of 1947 provided the framework for the modern planning system, which aimed to protect the greenbelt, while also providing housing and other community benefits. At the heart of it was the recognition that giving permission for land to be built on immediately makes it soar in value (this is known as 'betterment') and that these huge increases in value should be for the benefit of the community, for affordable housing, transport and other infrastructure, rather than just for individual landowners. The foundations of this approach were laid during the Second World War, in 1942, alongside the Beveridge Report of that year, which underpinned the future of the welfare state by taking aim at the five social evils of want, disease, ignorance, squalor and idleness. Beveridge described his famous report as 'one part only of a comprehensive policy of social progress'; another plank was contained in an accompanying 1942 report with the obscure title 'Final Report of the Expert Committee on Compensation and Betterment'.[6] This went on to form the basis of the postwar planning system and aimed to ensure that the huge profits made from the sale of land with planning permission would be used for community benefit, rather than just enriching landowners and fuelling a speculative market in land. This is not dissimilar to the principle that underpinned the success of the Garden Cities in the early part of the twentieth century, which is that they were able to take land at agricultural values and plough back the resulting profits from development into the community. Likewise, the New Towns built after the war and in the 1960s were kick-started by grants of land at agricultural value. This is broadly how the planning system operates in Germany and Holland.

The wartime authors of the report concluded that 'a means must be found for removing the conflict between private and public interest' and that this should be done by imposing a development charge, similar to a land tax, on landowners. This tax would siphon off the profits of soaring land values for local benefits. In keeping with the postwar ethos, the language of the report was shot through with the need to foster the public good, but the idea of a land tax is not limited to the left and has been promoted by such figures as Adam Smith, the eighteenth-century father of classical economic theory. Writing in *The Wealth of Nations* in 1776, Smith argued that a tax on 'ground rent' would prevent landowners from gaining monopolies. It took until 1909 for reforming Prime Minister Lloyd George to make the first attempt to introduce such a tax, with the backing of Churchill, who famously said: 'Roads are made ... electric light turns night into day . . . and all the while the landlord sits still . . . To not one of these improvements does the land monopolist . . . contribute, and yet by every one of them the value of his land is enhanced.'

Although many countries successfully use land taxes, the postwar system in the UK, which both compensated and taxed landowners, was complex and difficult to administer. It was abandoned by the Conservatives in 1954 after which successive Labour governments introduced variations of it, which were then dropped by the Tories. In 1967 Labour introduced a 'betterment levy' set at 40 per cent of profit, which was scrapped by Edward Heath in 1970, then Labour brought in a development land tax in 1975 set at 80 per cent of the increase in land value, which was maintained by the Thatcher government at 60 per cent. But in 1985 Nigel Lawson scrapped it, in tune with the spirit of the age and the deregulation of finance which came with 'Big Bang' a year later. The consequence is that the planning system is not working as its architects intended because one half of it, the tax mechanism to dampen speculation and provide benefits to the community, is no longer there. Meanwhile, the remaining half, which protects the greenbelt, restricts the amount of land available and makes it even more valuable.

Since the early 1990s there have been attempts to get developers to contribute to affordable housing under a clause in legislation called Section 106, also known as 'planning obligations'. This is a legal agreement between the local authority and the developer whereby the developer is required to contribute beneficial improvements to the local area in connection with its development, in particular affordable housing and infrastructure. Under this system, housebuilders are legally bound to work with local authorities to build a percentage of affordable housing in all new developments. Over the last generation some housing has been built in this way, but nowhere near the numbers needed, and the increasingly Orwellian definition of 'affordable' means that much of the small amount provided is far from affordable for most. This is particularly acute in London. In 2013 Mayor Boris Johnson's 'London Plan' redefined 'affordable rent' to mean up to 80 per cent of market rate, while the Housing and Planning Act 2016 deemed that affordable housing includes

Starter Homes for up to £450,000. These are not remotely affordable even to many people on relatively high incomes. Now even this has come under threat with the introduction of the 'viability assessment'. By making the costs of a scheme artificially high and undervaluing the final development, it can seem as though developers can hardly afford to build any 'affordable housing'. Housing academic Bob Colenutt says the viability assessment means developers 'have a new weapon to use – and are using it to devastating effect'.[7] These figures are all contained in Financial Viability Assessments, confidential reports developers supply to local authorities, based on little more than spurious figures and false accounting, in a process that Colenutt describes as 'extensive and open gaming of the system. It's out and out fraud.'

FINANCIAL VIABILITY

The Heygate Estate turned Elephant Park in Elephant and Castle is a good example of this. Previously secret information emerged following Freedom of Information requests in 2012 by local people campaigning against the lack of affordable housing in the development,[8] which were refused by the council but later granted by the Information Commissioner's Office in 2015, three years after the initial requests. The way a viability assessment works is by taking the total costs of a project and subtracting the projected revenue from sales of homes – which is lower if there is more affordable housing – and so calculating the rate of return which has to be deemed 'viable'. It's a system already stacked in favour of developers, especially in a rising market, as the projected revenue is based on existing land values and the viable rate of return is set at 20 per cent, which is the same as the performance fee for most hedge funds. This may have seemed a good incentive in the recessionary early 2000s when it was conceived, but doubling property prices since then means that today it equates to 100 per cent more profits. The figures are invariably calculated to maximize costs and minimize values. At Elephant Park, developer Lendlease employed the consultancy arm of estate agent Savills to carry out the calculations for them, with

Savills stating that the level of 'acceptable' profit should be 25 per cent. According to procedure, the council has to commission its own independent appraisal of the viability assessment by the government's District Valuer Service. This raised concerns about the 25 per cent level, but that made no difference to the outcome.*

The result was the replacement of 3,000 homes of predominantly social housing on the Heygate Estate with 2,704 luxury apartments, of which only eighty-two are social housing. The council accepted that eighty-two were all that was 'viable' for the developers. Like tax avoidance, this legalized evasion of the obligation to provide affordable housing is hidden by a total lack of transparency. When it comes to viability assessments, the cloak of commercial confidentiality is so powerful that not even the councillors on council planning committees are allowed to see the viability reports, although they are the democratically elected bodies which decide which schemes should go ahead and on what grounds. This subversion of the planning system is going on all over London and in other cities, and has spawned an entire industry of consultants around it. Savills may be one of the best known but there are hosts of others, including a company called S106 Management Ltd which had a graphic on its website describing the steps developers need to take to get out of providing affordable housing. In the first step a speech bubble asks, 'Do I really have to pay for, or provide affordable housing?' By the fifth cartoon a graphic shows how, after utilizing the company's expertise, the result is a wheelbarrow piled high with £ signs, and in the sixth image a palm tree is accompanied by the strapline, 'Go on a nice holiday with the money you've saved.'[9] The company also boasts case studies on its website of more than a dozen schemes where the requirement for affordable housing was dropped following their viability assessment.

The postwar planning system was conceived as a way of

---

* As to the way sales values were calculated, the Freedom of Information requests revealed that comparison properties which were looked at included a former council flat on the edge of the borough, which is not comparable at all with a centrally located luxury flat, as proved by actual sales values which rose to more than two thirds higher than projected.

maintaining a balance between restricting the land supply to protect the green belt and ensuring that the land that is provided meets the needs of the community, most of all through the provision of housing. But it has become, above all, a mechanism to increase the value of land. Developers pocket speculative increases in land values without providing the numbers or types of homes needed by local people. The quality of the homes built has little to do with property prices. The UK builds the smallest homes in Europe,[10] often to poor standards.[11] This is the result of a system which encourages competition between developers to focus first and foremost on acquiring the best land sites rather than on producing the best product. The desire of the super-rich to tear down and rebuild London property also reflects the financial reality that the important asset is the land, rather than the home itself.

The free market answer to the malfunctioning planning system is simply to remove it, loosening regulations as much as is politically possible to make it easier for developers to build more, smaller homes and therefore bring prices down. This is ridiculously simplistic. It's derided even by right-wing thinkers: a report from the Conservative think tank the Bow Group rejects the conventional wisdom of the property lobby that planning deregulation and government subsidies for lenders and buyers will solve the affordability crisis.[12] Report author Daniel Valentine writes: 'The solution is not extra supply. Extra supply feeds house price inflation, by reassuring investors that house price inflation will continue. The property lobby says that price is a function of supply and that increasing supply will eventually cut prices. The opposite is actually the case.' Conversely, he points out that when supply fell following the financial crisis, prices fell as well. Investment markets operate differently from user markets, with investors attracted to the rising prices which exclude users.[13] The unleashing of the market when it is not mediated by a planning system also creates dangerous speculative bubbles, as anyone who has looked at the property market in Spain or Ireland can see. There a deregulated market enabled the large-scale building of homes and was followed in both countries by a property crash, triggered by the financial crisis, resulting in millions of unsold, empty properties. Many British towns and cities also found themselves with a glut of empty apartments, and at the time of writing thousands of luxury apartments lie empty and unsold as the market cools. But the UK has so far largely avoided the Spanish and Irish experience, thanks in part to the regulation the planning system still imposes.

In England, the devotion to the green belt is likely to protect the planning system to a degree, but it is being loosened and undermined in every other respect. Planning is also where local people and local democracy meet and interact, with local communities at the heart of battles to keep some genuinely affordable housing. By law, communities have to be consulted about new plans for their areas, but consultations like the one on the Heygate are increasingly branded a sham, not dissimilar to Financial Viability Assessments in their failure to reflect the truth. But if this is one area where democracy is clearly and visibly failing, it is also perhaps the place where we can begin to revive it, as campaigners in Elephant and Castle are showing, challenging the idea that the solution to our crisis is to remove all regulation entirely. If we want housing to be a public good, we need more democratic control, not less.

FINANCIALIZATION

When Margaret Thatcher introduced Right to Buy, few people thought the aim was to get rid of council housing – there was simply too much of it. The intention, continued under Labour, was to transfer control of millions of council homes to housing associations, in a process known as 'stock transfer' – which critics claim is privatization through the back door. Housing associations are also known as Registered Social Landlords, and in the 1990s, council housing underwent its first major linguistic change and became known as 'social housing'.

With their roots in the Victorian charitable and voluntary sector and represented by organizations such as the philanthropic Peabody Trust, housing associations were in a tradition of social provision that appealed to Conservative thinking. The Thatcher government also abolished rent controls, which had been in place since 1915, deregulated the private rented sector and created the framework for the introduction of Buy to Let, all of which contribute to today's housing crisis.

These policies began with the Conservatives but only really got going under Tony Blair's New Labour government. When New Labour swept to power in 1997 the government rolled out its 'Decent Homes' agenda, aimed at transferring 200,000 homes a year to housing associations, pledging investment and refurbishment as a condition of transfer. Foreshadowing today's democratic deficit, while the policy was supposed to be dependent on the majority of tenants voting in favour of transfer and reflecting 'tenants' choice', when tenants began voting 'no', the process became mired in controversy and accusations of ballot rigging.* Many of the transfers happened in the end,† and, according to housing academic Paul Watt, Decent Homes 'ensured marketization either directly or indirectly by ruling out direct public investment by councils in their stock'.[14]

While housing has long undergone a process of stealth privatization, this accelerated sharply in 2010 when the Conservative-led coalition came to power, at least in part because many leading Tories simply don't believe in social housing. In 2016, I was invited to speak at the Housing Studies Association annual conference, where I shared a platform with Chris Walker, the director of housing at Policy Exchange, the Conservative think tank which feeds directly into Conservative policymaking. During an angry question and answer session a member of the audience asked Chris if social housing remained 'the right answer in our times', to which Chris replied that the 'social rent straitjacket is symptomatic to the postwar construct'.

* Glasgow and Birmingham city councils and many London councils voted 'no', with campaign groups such as Defend Council Housing, trade unions and elements within the Labour Party claiming stock transfer was the privatization of public housing, although the then Labour government insisted it was modernization.

† In keeping with the spirit of the times, the Private Finance Initiative was another option councils were allowed to consider in order to meet Decent Homes standards – which has had similar unpalatable consequences to the use of PFI in the NHS.

Despite the opaque wording this sounded like a 'no' to me and chimes very much with what I've heard from a number of senior Tories. An adviser to a senior Conservative politician explained his vision to me, arguing that social housing undermines dignity, self-respect and aspiration and that even if it meant ameliorating the housing crisis they would not wish to return to the era of large-scale social housing provision.

The contradictions of today's planning system and the failure of the housing market to provide anything like the number of homes people need have preoccupied successive governments for the last twenty years. The most notable attempt to find solutions was when Gordon Brown as Chancellor of the Exchequer appointed Bank of England economist Kate Barker to head up a review of housing supply in 2003. The conundrum the Treasury was wrestling with was why the private sector was failing to respond to the demand for more homes. The reason is very simple: housebuilders have greater guarantees of profits if they limit supply and keep prices high, taking maximum advantage of the restrictions in land supply imposed by the planning system. This is why the free market answer to the problem is the wrong one: it fails to account for community needs. Housebuilders are not to be blamed in this: they are private companies whose first priority is to provide maximum returns for their shareholders. Instead, it is central government which has relinquished responsibility by effectively removing any mechanism to get developers to share the massive profits they make with local communities.

Barker reached a similar conclusion in her interim report, where she noted that in order to maximize their profits, developers control the rate of production and 'trickle out' no more than 100–200 houses a year from a large development. 'This may not be desirable from society's point of view,' she wrote.[15] But by the time the final review came out six months later, the role of developers in limiting supply had been airbrushed out. Instead, the main recommendation was that the solution to the housing crisis was to remove restrictions on the planning system, to encourage developers to build in such large numbers that prices would come down. The final report also recommended that the government spend between £1.2 billion and £1.6 billion annually to fund social housing and that a new 'planning gain supplement' be introduced[16] – but neither saw the light of day. Since Gordon Brown failed to heed Kate Barker's warning of how housebuilders trickle out homes, no governing party has challenged the monopoly the top housebuilders have over the industry.

When he was Leader of the Opposition in 2014, Ed Miliband identified similar issues and criticized developers for 'land banking', the process whereby housebuilders buy up land and fail to build on it as they wait for it to rise in value. An investigation by the *Guardian* found that Britain's biggest housebuilders are sitting on enough land with planning permission to create more than 600,000 new homes. Berkeley, Barratt, Persimmon and Taylor Wimpey, the four biggest companies in the industry, own more than three quarters of the plots, and give over £1.5 billion to shareholders.[17] Miliband threatened that under a Labour government, developers would have to 'use it or lose it', declaring that 'we've got to break the power of the big developers because they're sitting on hundreds of thousands of places for homes with planning permission and not building because they're waiting for it to accumulate in value.'[18] In 2016, Secretary of State for Communities Sajid Javid echoed these concerns in a keynote speech to housebuilders, telling them that: 'I cannot look the other way when I see land banking holding up development. Some of you have conceded to me, in private, that it happens. Some of you still deny it's an issue. But there's clearly something going on. The number of plots approved for residential development each year rose by 59 per cent between 2011 and 2015. But the number of building starts rose by just 29 per cent.'[19] But despite these threats very little has happened to stop the practice, and the stranglehold of the developers continues. When the government published its Housing White Paper in 2017 it proposed the maximum amount of time developers are allowed to land bank be reduced from three years to two, but with caveats, leading to criticisms that this will be difficult to implement.

Instead, in urging the removal of planning restrictions, the Conservatives appear to be hoping for a return to the 1930s, before we had a functioning planning system and the private sector produced the classic 1930s semi-detached houses which define London's sprawling metroland suburbs – and which gave impetus to calls for a greenbelt. Between 1935 and 1936, the private sector hit a peak, building 279,000 homes, before it settled into its postwar pattern of around 150,000 per year, alongside the 100,000 council homes provided until Margaret Thatcher came to power. But removing planning restrictions not only risks the creation of ruinous housing bubbles, in the UK it is almost politically impossible to substantially remove restrictions on the greenbelt – which Conservative voters in particular are very keen to defend. The consequence is that, even if nearly all meaningful restrictions on the planning system are removed within London and other cities hit by the housing crisis, land supply will remain tight and land prices, fuelled by global capital, will continue to be high, even allowing for a significant downturn in the market. This is the context for the enthusiasm behind the demolition of so many of London's housing estates, as policymakers identify these substantial parts of the city as the only large sites available for new housing, regardless of the collateral damage to communities.

Much of the 'affordable' housing in new developments now includes the 'starter homes' valued at up to £450,000 in London and £250,000 outside the capital. So far, all the evidence shows that this policy adds further inflationary pressure on land and property prices, creating a ripple effect of high prices which displaces residents. Building these expensive starter homes also means that genuinely affordable and social rented homes won't be built, with the Local Government Association pointing out that the government's own analysis suggests that, if 100,000 starter homes are built through the planning system, between 56,000 and 71,000 social and affordable rented homes will not be built.[20]

So while people are in desperate need of housing, housebuilders are laughing all the way to the bank. Research by Sheffield Hallam University analysing the financial records of the biggest housebuilders found that end-of-year profits for the five biggest firms rose from £372 million in 2010 to over £2 billion by 2015, a staggering increase of over 480 per cent.[21] At the same time, dividend payments to shareholders in 2015 amounted to 43 per cent of yearly profits, raising significant questions about the levels of reinvestment in housing production taking place.[22] If ever a clear sign were needed of the extent to which the original aims of the planning system have been distorted, then this is it. Community benefit has made way for profits of billions for the housebuilders.

When Theresa May replaced David Cameron as prime minister, her government signalled a shift away from the ideologically driven emphasis on allowing free rein to the excesses of the market; Sajid Javid's comments on land banking reflect this, although in essence much remains the same. May has also moved away from the focus on home ownership, a pragmatic response to a policy which is clearly not working, given home ownership continues to fall. In place of this comes renewed concentration on the private rented market. Unfortunately, the housing crisis is at least as severe here. Neither are attempts to reboot the private rented sector new: the coalition government launched a review into it – headed by Sir Adrian Montague, who pioneered the use of the Private Finance Initiative – which resulted in a £1.1 billion Build to Rent fund. So far, initiatives like this have failed to make a difference despite repeated government efforts.* Ironically, one of the reasons for this, which the government itself has highlighted, is that investors may be attracted by secure, longer-term tenancies such as those in Germany, Switzerland and the Netherlands;[23] at six months, the UK has the shortest legal minimum for tenancies in the world, paralleled only by Australia. Even the US ensures tenancies must be at least a year long.[24] Yet when the Labour Party suggested in 2015 that the standard tenancy should be three years, the government responded that would mean 'strangling the sector with unnecessary rules and red tape'.[25] In many ways ideological commitment on the right remains alive and well.

Resistance to regulation and rampant financialization also

* The UK is home to the smallest corporate residential rental sector among comparable advanced capitalist countries, with institutional investment accounting for less than 1 per cent.

characterize the one part of the private rental market that investors *are* increasingly interested in, which is student housing. Purpose-built student accommodation is listed on the London Stock Exchange through 'tax efficient' financial vehicles known as REITS.* In recent years, these have transformed this part of the market. A report by property consultants Savills describes 'the flowering of student housing' as it has grown from 'a niche investment opportunity to a global asset class', with the UK by far the most popular home for global institutional and private capital, attracting almost $9 billion in the last three years. Student accommodation in London is also the most expensive in the world. At $1,600 per month,[26] which is more than the value of a year's student loan, it limits it largely to wealthy and overseas students. The consequence is that almost half of students have to try their luck in the private rented sector and rent strikes are becoming a regular feature of London campuses. Everything outlined above is the result of opening up every aspect of housing to the market, from accommodation for students with limited resources to social housing which is no longer a non-profit sector.†

Even claims that local authorities are to build council homes once again turn out to be little more than a smokescreen, as councils set up companies that act as commercial developers, often in partnership with lucrative investment vehicles which will leave tenants paying higher rents. For example, in Barking and Dagenham, regarded as a successful model that many other councils are trying to emulate, the council formed a Special Purpose Vehicle (SPV) called Reside with financing from a company called Long Harbour, which developed housing on the basis of a sixty-year lease. This enabled the council to argue that the scheme is not a sell-off of housing because they retain the freehold. Long Harbour pay the council an allowance for management and maintenance of the properties, but they get to keep all of the rental income until the company's investment (plus interest) is repaid. And because the council is under pressure to maximize its

* Real estate investment trusts

† Following the introduction of a little-known clause in the Housing and Regeneration Act, which slipped in unnoticed in 2009, profit-making companies can register as affordable housing providers.

returns to Long Harbour, very few social homes have been built. As for Long Harbour, it financed the project through another linked company, called Atlantic Regeneration Trust, registered offshore for tax purposes. The chief executive of Long Harbour is one William Waldorf Astor IV, who is Samantha Cameron's half-brother.

Now Lambeth is planning to create an SPV (which will include a group of companies seeking investment), called 'Homes for Lambeth', and has appointed Savills to advise the council on how to set it up. But many local residents are concerned, especially on Cressingham Gardens which the council plans to demolish, claiming it can build more council homes on the estate through the SPV. The council's argument is that in this way they can effectively act as a property developer, using profits they will make from building 511 new homes – including 301 on social rents – for the benefit of Lambeth residents. 'With the council acting as a commercial developer through Homes for Lambeth we can use the 15–20 per cent development surplus that private developers normally make and reinvest this into our communities and build more homes for local people,' the council states on its website.[27] But, as in Barking and Dagenham, the SPV is a private equity company accountable to shareholders. Campaigners claim there are no guarantees that it will keep rents low or ensure homes remain in the public sector. Local resident Pam Douglas points out that under this model the council assumes all the risk while shareholders walk away with the dividends. Although very little public information is available, there are fears that its structure will be similar to the public private partnerships and private finance initiatives which have placed hospitals, schools and housing in crippling debt for decades to come. More than a third of UK local authorities are setting up their own housing companies, such as Homes for Lambeth and Brick by Brick in Croydon. The business model is to build a mix of homes for private sale which will subsidize council homes, but the concern is just how many social homes will be built and how affordable they will turn out to be.

Another company hoping to take advantage of the profits that can now be made from social housing was New York-based private equity firm Westbrook Partners, which hit the headlines when it bought the New Era Estate in Hackney in 2014. Originally built in the 1930s by a charitable trust in Hoxton, the estate provided homes for working-class Londoners. When Westbrook took over they offered tenants the chance to stay as long as they could meet the new 'normalized' rents, which meant an increase of 400 per cent. The company served eviction notices in the run-up to Christmas, stepped into a huge media storm and was forced to back down, before transferring the estate to a charitable landlord.

Westbrook is what academic Stuart Hodkinson describes as an 'archetypal Global Corporate Landlord', a private equity firm which raises capital from large institutions such as pension funds and insurance companies to leverage further loans from banks and capital markets in order to pursue high-risk and high-return investments in real estate. The US private equity firm Blackstone is the largest Global Corporate Landlord in the world,[28] and has specialized in buying up housing and commercial real estate in what are known as 'distressed markets' in the US, Spain, Ireland and Greece, following the financial crash. In the US many of the repossessed homes bought by Blackstone have found their way into its rental subsidiary, Invitation Homes, which controls about 50,000 homes. Overall, American institutional investors own around half a million family homes.[29] This may sound a small figure, but as rental property becomes a major new asset class, especially if property prices fall and mortgage credit dries up – not unlikely in London – these are trends we are very possibly to see much more of.

Blackstone and other Global Corporate Landlords, such as Goldman Sachs, have been the focus of international protests, culminating in a series of global days of action, under the banner of #StopBlackstone Our Homes Are not a Commodity.[30] The anger was caused by the sale of almost 5,000 rent-controlled apartments in Madrid to Goldman Sachs and Blackstone, accompanied by the by now familiar broken promises that rents would remain the same. Instead, as old contracts expired, people were told rents would increase dramatically and were threatened with eviction or moved out to escape the insecurity. One mother described how her rent went up from €58 to €436, which was taken out of her bank account without her knowledge.[31] London has not yet witnessed the same property market collapse which made these such good deals for Global Corporate Landlords but, as for other UK towns and cities, a full-scale crash remains a possibility and the capital's rental market is poised to become an increasingly attractive asset class to institutional investors given the government's indication of more support for Build to Rent. Blackstone, with its UK headquarters in Mayfair's Berkeley Square, is very well placed to play a leading role.

Now, on top of all this comes the Housing and Planning Act, seen as the final nail in the coffin for social housing and bitterly opposed by a wide coalition of campaigners from 'Kill the Bill' housing activist groups, who organized demonstrations of tens of thousands through central London, to figures at the heart of the establishment, such as Sir Bob Kerslake, the former head of the civil service. The campaign by Labour, Lib Dem and cross bench peers in the House of Lords inflicted eighteen successive defeats on the government, managing to water down some of the most egregious excesses. Theresa May's government has removed some of the emphasis on providing expensive starter homes, but the death knell for social housing rings loud and clear. Writing in the *Guardian* after the bill passed into law in 2016, Kerslake said: 'I have reluctantly come to the conclusion that for the leading figures in this government, publicly provided, social rented housing is now seen as toxic. This is something that I deeply regret.'[32] In 2017, Theresa May's government published its own statement about housing policy in its Housing White Paper, which made no mention at all of housing for social rent.

One of the key proposals to hit tenants as a result of the Housing and Planning Act is the end of lifetime tenancies, largely replaced by fixed-term tenancies of two to five years. This means that at the end of this period people will have to move into the private rented sector, because there is so little social housing available. Meanwhile, research from the Chartered Institute of Housing predicts that the benefit cap, which has been lowered to £23,000 a year in London and £20,000 outside and came into force in 2016, will affect 116,000 families with 300,000 children, leaving them unable to afford rents and at risk of eviction and homelessness. In London the institute found 18,000 families were likely to be affected.[33] At the same time as the livelihoods of families on benefits are undermined, the Act gives councils a duty to promote the supply of the £450,000 starter homes.

The Act also grants automatic planning permission for brownfield sites, including housing estates, paving the way for widespread demolitions. These have already started to redefine London. It opens the door to the direct privatizing of local authority planning by allowing developers to choose private sector consultancies, rather than local authorities, to process planning applications in pilot areas. This further undermines the democratic accountability of council planning departments. Planning academics describe the Act as no less than 'an attempt to destroy any form of democratic control of planning and land use'.[34]

The failure of the democratic process cuts to the core of the Housing and Planning Act, but for me the clearest indication of the contempt in which democracy is held in this vital area of our lives came with the third reading of the bill in the House of Commons. Although this was the final chance for MPs to debate a highly contentious bill of enormous interest to the general public, the debate was held in to the early hours of the morning. Despite calls from opposition MPs to reschedule, it did not begin until 9 p.m., ending at 2 a.m. Fiona Mactaggart, Labour MP for Slough, said: 'There are a number of really important issues which, frankly, I think our constituents, who are concerned about housing and planning, would not expect to be decided after midnight.' It also emerged that sixty-five pages of new clauses – amounting to almost a third of the bill – had been tabled at the last minute, most of which were to be considered by MPs for the first time. Roberta Blackman-Woods, Labour MP for Durham, described the debacle as 'simply appalling and means that there will be no proper scrutiny of almost a third of the bill'.[35] Steve Topple, a journalist covering the bill's passage for the *Independent*, described how the late-night debate was characterized by 'the sound of guffawing Tories and the constant background tinkling of MPs achieving high scores on Candy Crush. I kid you not.'[36]

3
Demolitions

ELEPHANT PARK

'I've got a friend of mine – Terry – he could only afford to move out of the area with what the council was offering him and ended up moving into a home somewhere just outside Sidcup. Terry's probably in his late fifties and he lives with his wife. He's lived here all his life. He's got people that would see him on a daily basis and his family lives here in the area. He's now living there isolated just outside Sidcup having broken all of his social ties, he's now suffering from severe depression . . . It's not easy to build new social ties, especially the older you are . . . I mean the number of people I heard who've passed away as a result of having to move . . . for me, it's genocide.'[1]

Terry used to live on the Heygate Estate in Elephant and Castle, which has now been replaced by Elephant Park, the new development by the Australian developer Lendlease, which includes 2,704 predominantly luxury apartments, of which only eighty-two are for social housing.* As for the majority of the properties, at the time of writing a two-bedroom apartment on Elephant Park cost anything between £750,000 and £1 million, with 100 per cent of the apartments in the first phase sold to foreign investors.[2] What has happened on the Heygate is not an isolated incident. Estates all over London, from east to west and south to north, are tipped for demolition in a process that

---

* Twenty-five per cent are for 'affordable housing' but since this was redefined by the Conservatives to mean either up to 80 per cent of market rent or starter homes to buy for £450,000, this is far from affordable even to Londoners on far above average incomes.

Beverley, one of the last remaining residents in Chiltern Block on the Aylesbury Estate. Since the start of the dispute between the council and residents and campaigners, the block has become known as 'Alcatraz'.

advocates describe as 'estate regeneration' and critics condemn as social cleansing. As communities are broken up and tens of thousands of people displaced, this is another defining feature of London's housing crisis. Down the road in Elephant and Castle tenants and homeowners on the Aylesbury Estate are fighting eviction. Neighbouring Lambeth Council has plans to demolish three estates and partially demolish three more.* The list goes on: the Carpenters Estate and Robin Hood Gardens in East London, which is internationally acclaimed as a modernist masterpiece; Woodberry Down in North London and the Silchester Estate and Alton Estate in West London. In Haringey the council has agreed to proceed with a controversial £2 billion plan with Lendlease that will include the demolition of Northumberland Park. These are just a handful of the hundreds of estates either already demolished or under consideration for demolition, to be replaced by developments of largely luxury apartments which the government argues have increased the overall total numbers of housing, although the amount of social housing has fallen sharply.[3] Paul Watt, urban studies academic at Birkbeck College, believes that, on the basis of existing plans, estate demolition is affecting more than 100 estates – a figure which does not include all the proposals currently being drawn up. London councils own on average 25 to 30 per cent of the land in their boroughs – Southwark owns 43 per cent and Islington about a third. Lord Adonis, chair of the National Infrastructure Commission, has stated that he wishes to see London's 3,500 housing estates undergo 'systematic estate regeneration'[4] – which housing activists claim could displace hundreds of thousands of people.

Soon after the EU referendum, I drove to the outskirts of London to see Terry and his wife, Brenda. Bexley was strongly Leave territory with 75 per cent voting to leave the EU and St George's flags hanging out of the windows in the surrounding streets. Before they were forced out in 2008, Terry and Brenda, who are now in their late sixties, lived on the Heygate for thirty-four years. Terry, a retired

---

* Lambeth identified six estates as part of its 'estate regeneration' programme with the decision taken to demolish Cressingham Gardens, Central Hill and the Fenwick Estate and to partially demolish and redevelop Knights Walk, the Westbury Estate and the South Lambeth Estate.

facilities manager, described to me how they had moved into their three-bedroom flat in 1974 when the estate, which was home to 3,000 people, opened. 'It was virtually day one, it was a brand-new flat. We had the kids' childhood and their schooling there, to the point they started work. We had facilities – a crèche which my wife was involved in running, youth clubs – it was a close-knit community.' They bought the flat under the Right to Buy in 1986, though Terry had mixed feelings about it. 'I was very anti the sell-off of council homes but I thought I'd be in there till the day I died. There was no reason to think otherwise.'

In 2008, they were offered £168,000 for their flat by Southwark Council, which had issued a Compulsory Purchase Order against them and the remaining leaseholders on the estate. Although their own independent surveyor valued the flat at considerably more, they were advised to settle on a slightly higher final offer of £172,000. Speaking at the public inquiry into the circumstances surrounding the compulsory purchase of the properties, Terry said: 'I could no longer afford to stay in the area – the compensation I was offered plus £45,000 of life savings bought me a terraced property fifteen miles out of London. I have been forced to give up my home to accommodate the building of homes for overseas investors.' This was despite pledges by Southwark Council that residents would be given like-for-like replacement of their homes within the borough, and the council promising that the regeneration 'offers a rare opportunity to build new homes for all Heygate tenants in the Elephant and Castle area'.[5] Instead, research shows that the majority of Heygate tenants no longer live in Southwark, pushed to outlying parts of London, with families uprooted and children taken out of their schools. As for residents who owned their own homes, most of them have had to leave London altogether as prices offered by the council for the compulsory purchase of properties were so low, pushing people out as far as Sevenoaks, Thurrock and Rochester.[6] According to Freedom of Information requests the average compulsory purchase price was £95,480 for a one-bedroom flat and £107,230 for two beds.[7] A significant number of people, like Terry, forced to leave family, friends and social networks, became depressed and several older residents died during the process.

Many residents and opponents of the council's plans believed that soaring land values in the area were the main driver, but the deal with Lendlease remained obscure as the council claimed it was 'too commercially sensitive' for it to release any information – until embarrassingly an edited version of the confidential agreement was uploaded on to the Southwark Council website by mistake. The document, which was quickly removed, had sensitive sections blacked out, but an error meant it was possible to copy and paste the redacted words. This showed that, having spent £44 million emptying the 22-acre estate, Lendlease paid the council only £50 million for it, a price more than ten times below market value, as reflected by a nearby 1.5-acre site which sold at a similar time for £40 million.[8]

For Terry and Brenda, the most significant impact of what happened has been the psychological effect of the break-up of the community. 'It was devastating. My wife's family had been in the area for a hundred years. We had in the region of thirty family members in Elephant and Castle. There's one left on the Aylesbury Estate – and she won't be there much longer,' Terry said. 'I was born in Elephant and Castle and I'd always lived around the area,' Brenda explained. 'Mum and Dad were Bermondsey born and bred, my grandparents, everyone. Southwark was our place.' The health impacts are the most clearly visible. Pulling up his trousers Terry showed me mottled, swollen legs, covered in eczema, which seemed to belong to a much older man. 'Until I moved out I'd never had any of these issues or even been to hospital. Now I have high blood pressure and blood clots on the lung. I'm on about seven tablets a day. The doctors say stress is a part of it.' As for Brenda, since the move she's been in a wheelchair. She also has a liver condition, requiring frequent appointments at Guy's and St Thomas' Hospital in central London. Fifteen minutes from where they used to live, it is now an hour and a half commute for them. 'It's taken me years to get over the shock. I've got neighbours here but I haven't got friends. My friends from London come up once a month but I used to see them every day,' Brenda told me, sitting with her iPad in her lap opened to Facebook. 'This is my friend now,' she said.

Because the same themes are now playing out all around London, it is worth looking closely at what happened at the Heygate, which was identified as part of an 'opportunity area' for growth in the late 1990s at the same time as it became clear that the homes themselves needed investment. Consequently, the council commissioned a report which concluded that the buildings were structurally sound but in need of complete refurbishment and some partial demolition. It also found that 'the crime statistics show a very low crime rate for this estate' and a larger than average proportion of elderly people with a significant attachment to the place. The recommendations were for some demolition of the tower blocks and refurbishment of the rest as the most cost-effective solution, environmentally, architecturally and socially.[9]

But in 2002, a council document identified the Heygate as 'a barrier to releasing the area's potential',[10] which put in motion the council's plans to demolish it. Using language that a PR company might today have told him to avoid, Southwark's then director of regeneration, Fred Manson, didn't mince his words, arguing that the area needed a different kind of demographic to prosper. 'We need to have a wider range of people living in the borough ... social housing generates people on low incomes coming in and that generates poor school performances, middle-class people stay away.'[11] He explained that 'above thirty per cent [of the population in need] it becomes pathological'[12] and claimed that 'we're trying to move people from a benefit dependency culture to an enterprise culture',[13] although just getting people to move seemed the main aim as far as the growing number of activists and campaigners were concerned. In 2008, Lendlease were named lead developers. The council's promise of managed but 'inclusive gentrification'[14] soon fell apart as barely any of the promised new homes were built by the time the majority moved out. As the estate emptied and became characterized by boarded-up properties, the Heygate was portrayed by the council as a dangerous and crime-ridden sink estate, justifying the demolition. The media ran with the story, with a BBC piece headlined 'Muggers' "paradise", the Heygate Estate is demolished'.[15] Reflecting a mainstream media narrative

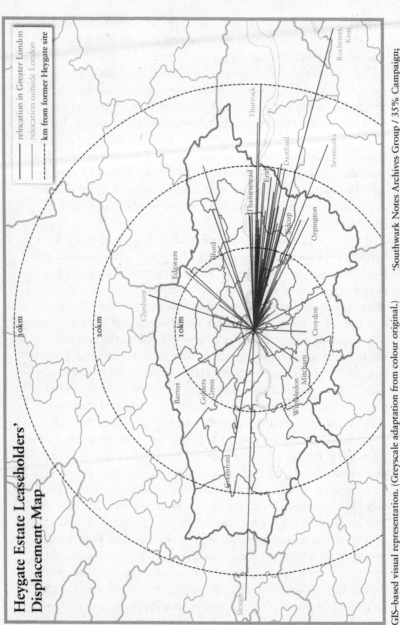

Heygate Estate Leaseholders'
Displacement Map

relocation in Greater London
relocation outside London
km from former Heygate site

30km

20km

10km

Cheshunt

Edgware

Ilford

Thamesmead

Thurrock

Erith

Dartford

Sevenoaks

Sidcup

Orpington

Rochester, Kent.

Barnet

Golders Green

Wimbledon

Mitcham

Croydon

Greenford

Slough

GIS–based visual representation. (Greyscale adaptation from colour original.)

'Southwark Notes Archives Group / 35% Campaign;
www.southwarknotes.wordpress.com / www.35percent.org

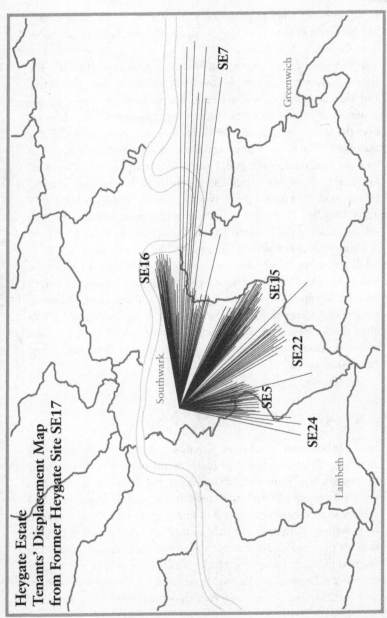

**Heygate Estate
Tenants' Displacement Map
from Former Heygate Site SE17**

SE7

SE16

SE15

SE22

SE5

SE24

Greenwich

Southwark

Lambeth

GIS-based visual representation. (Greyscale adaptation from colour original.)

'Southwark Notes Archives Group / 35% Campaign;
www.southwarknotes.wordpress.com / www.35percent.org

which bore no relation to actual crime figures, such commentary has become familiar to estate residents all over London opposing demolitions.

I had gone to see Terry and Brenda a few days after the EU referendum, when few people could talk about anything else. Terry and Brenda had both voted Leave, like most of their new neighbours – the vast majority of whom moved out from inner London over the last generation. But in their case, they both think the way they were treated by Southwark Council informed their decision. 'We got badly let down and I wanted a different view. We were Londoners. I was so happy there – perhaps it was sour grapes,' Brenda said. 'The more I think about it, I think, "did we vote right?"' Terry wonders. 'But then I think of a Labour-controlled borough selling us down the line and Labour council leader Peter John hob-nobbing with developers in Cannes, and he's trying to preach to us while living in a luxury development in Tower Bridge. It's about not having choices. They've drained you of all your finances. I wasn't looking for profit, I was just looking for a home. And I know of people who were offered less than us.' For Terry and Brenda it was clear that at least the EU referendum seemed to give them a choice, where previously all choice and all control over their future had been taken away.

'ALCATRAZ'

Now, Labour-run Southwark Council is hoping to demolish the Aylesbury Estate, designed to house 7,500 people. It shot to fame in 1997 when Tony Blair chose it as the location for his first speech as prime minister and stood in the middle of the estate to declare that 'the poorest people in our country have been forgotten by government'. In 2015, the fight to save the Aylesbury from demolition hit the headlines when Occupy protesters occupied empty flats for two months. Today, the blocks which were part of the Occupy protest are known as 'Alcatraz' because of the twenty-foot wooden and metal-spiked fences and checkpoint-style entrance. I'd heard about Alcatraz and wanted to see it, so I walked through the estate to the Alcatraz blocks, past graffiti stencilled on the walls reading 'another s**t deal by Southwark Council' and 'big fat profits for property developers'. Perhaps as a punishment for the protesters, or so it is regarded as a deterrent, Alcatraz bears no resemblance to any regeneration scheme I have ever seen, not least one which still houses residents. I was told residents were allowed to enter or leave Alcatraz only through a single guarded entrance, which means a walk of half a mile for people who live furthest away from the gate. This is difficult for the elderly or disabled. When I finally arrived, the security guard refused to let me in because I didn't have permission from the council.

My second attempt to visit Alcatraz, to see Beverley Robinson, chair of the Aylesbury Leaseholders Action Group and one of the last remaining residents, was, if anything, more forbidding than the first. By now familiar with the single-entry checkpoint, I told the security guard who I was there to see, but to my surprise he told me the entrance was on another part of the estate. I tried in vain to find it, went back to the guard, who sent me away again, all the while getting later for my appointment. Eventually I found another part of the fence where a guard was sitting about thirty yards away, which meant I had to shout across the expanse numerous times before he let me in. When I told Beverley how difficult it had been to find her, she said that was standard practice: her friends were frequently misdirected, the postcode had been removed and the postman was told that no one lived there any more.

'People no longer come to visit because the fence is so unattractive and they get so much abuse from the security guards,' she said, adding that she has had scores of emails about the fence from residents coming home who can't get in. 'Then they [the council] say they're trying to protect me – who are they trying to protect me from?', she continued, referring to the council's disputed claim that the security was there to protect residents after they had asked for it. She agrees that the fence went up as a result of the Occupy protest, which was not the sort of experience Beverley, who worked as a post office manager for twenty-nine years, was used to, or took part in. The occupation lasted between February and March 2015, the police finally evicting protesters at the beginning of April. 'My aim was to get a fair value for my home. I didn't get involved but they did what they had to do. They're the foot soldiers on the ground, but that kind of campaign is not for me. I couldn't break into a flat and sleep rough in there – I don't even like going camping. But it put the Aylesbury on the map and showed solidarity.' When I left, she walked me back to the checkpoint where I'd been refused entry and asked the guard why he hadn't let me in. Although earlier he had repeatedly, and rudely, said I couldn't go in, now he kept saying he hadn't refused me entry, but had just told me to go a different way. It was Kafkaesque and unpleasant to find myself on the receiving end of behaviour Beverley and her neighbours have to put up with on a daily basis.

Beverley has lived in her flat for thirty years and bought it under the Right to Buy in 2005, just months before the council announced its intention to demolish. 'It's so ironic – it was misrepresentation. I'd saved up quite a bit, put my savings in and paid the rest in mortgage.' She has been locked in a battle with the council since 2010, when she was offered just £110,000 for her two-bedroom flat, subsequently revalued at £117,000. Either figure makes it impossible for her to buy another similar property in central London. Consequently she set up the Aylesbury Leaseholders Action Group, which has unearthed jaw-dropping information about just how little the council paid homeowners for their properties. Freedom of Information requests by another homeowner on the estate revealed that the council bought nearly forty properties for less than £100,000, with nine homes achieving values of less than £75,000 and the lowest coming in at £55,000, £57,000 and £63,000.[16] It is important to note that the council is legally bound to offer a fair market value and, although this tends to be a bone of contention as the value taken is that of a property on an already condemned estate, it is beyond doubt that these prices bear no relation to the value of land in this part of central London.

'People ask me, why did I start this – it's not because I want to be famous, it's because of the injustice,' Beverley told me. 'Most people are not going to fight them in court so they just cut their losses and go, but I said no.' The action group residents want to stay in their own homes, but as the council is determined to plough ahead with the demolition all they can do is struggle to get enough for their homes to stay in the area, or at the very least in London. After she appeared on BBC's *Inside Out* programme in 2014 Beverley received a revised offer of £187,000 – which is still £300,000 less than the £487,000 the housing association Notting Hill Housing Trust is asking for a two-bed flat in the proposed new development that will replace the Aylesbury. Not only is she nowhere near being able to afford one of the new homes, she is also priced out of the complex array of options the council claims are open to her, such as 'shared ownership' or 'shared equity', which come with high outgoings including service charges. Given that, the only choice she is left with is that the council buy back her property and rehouse her as a social housing tenant elsewhere, leaving her to spend the life savings she put into her home on paying rent.

In 2015 a public inquiry into the Compulsory Purchase Orders in the Alcatraz blocks took place, with the widespread expectation that the secretary of state would support the council's decision to demolish. While residents waited almost a year to find out their fate, they faced what many claimed was continual harassment by the council. Virtually no maintenance was carried out, fire escapes were sealed off, there was no lighting in the stairwells, the heating and gas were cut off and the bins were not emptied. 'I had no heating for weeks and weeks and then they wouldn't let the people in to fix it. One evening I came home and saw the gas man at the gate. I heard him saying to the guard, "They're so mean, they know people are living here and they're cutting off the gas." ' When she took it up with the council, she was told that it had been a mistake as they didn't think anyone was still using gas. On the very day the public inquiry decision was made known, Toby Eckersley, the former leader of the Tory group on Southwark Council and until recently a councillor for thirty-three years, felt compelled to write to Southwark after Beverley found herself with no electricity, no internet access, no hot water or heating and no lift services, which she was told was due to ongoing works. In his email to head of regeneration Mark Williams, Eckersley wrote:

> You need to be aware of the intolerable loss of basic services to which Beverley Robinson has been subject . . . She is not in the best of health, and because of the electricity failures is often unable to communicate by email or charge her phone. Even when the electricity is on it is imprudent to use the lift for fear of loss of power which would entail hours stuck in the lift.[. . .]
>
> It seems to me that the council, whether by act or omission, is behaving disgracefully, and unlawfully, towards its lessee and is at risk of severe reputational damage and litigation costs.

But what started out as a bad day turned into a surprisingly good one when, confounding all expectations, it was announced that on the advice of the Planning Inspector, Secretary of State for Communities and Local Government Sajid Javid would not confirm the Compulsory Purchase Order, on the basis that it breached the human rights of the leaseholders, according to Article 8 of the European Convention on Human Rights, which protects a person's 'right to respect for his private and family life, his home' and states that 'there shall be no interference by a public authority with the exercise of this right'. But the judgment did not just have recourse to European law, finding that the CPO also breached the Equality Act 2010 as the majority of those affected were from black or minority ethnic backgrounds. In her recommendation the inspector highlighted that 'the compulsory purchase order would not only deprive them of their dwelling but also their financial security. If they chose not to pursue this option, they would inevitably need to leave the area and this would have implications for their family life, including the lives of those dependent on them.' This was a huge victory for the residents and a testament to the strength of their campaign and the widespread support it received, with expert witnesses giving their time *pro bono*. But the fight is nowhere near over. The council appealed the decision in the High Court, where they lost, and at the time of writing they had announced their intention to appeal that decision, which means the running battle between council and leaseholders will continue to blight the lives of residents, with all that entails. When Beverley phoned me to tell me the news of the secretary of state's decision, she said she was 'ecstatic', but she also told me that the council's response to the electricity failure in her block was to give her a torch.

The struggle, which has so far lasted twelve years and looks set to continue, is bringing together unlikely bedfellows, from Occupy protesters to Toby Eckersley, who has been one of Beverley's staunchest supporters. A keen Thatcherite and prominent backer of the Tory flagship policy of Right to Buy, which cemented Margaret Thatcher in power and resulted in the sale of more than 2 million council homes, Eckersley stepped down from Southwark Council, where he had led the Conservative group, in 2014, by which time he had become involved with the leaseholders. Homeowners like Beverley and Terry on the Heygate, who exercised the Right to Buy, are known as leaseholders. Like so many homeowners in the UK, they own the leasehold of their property, while in this case the council retains the freehold, which is central to ownership rights and will be looked at later in this chapter.

'Most of the resident leaseholders I know best on the Aylesbury bought as a result of the Right to Buy because they wanted a home for life. Between 2001 and 2005 the council was actually preparing quite good plans to refurbish the estate, so they had every reason to believe it would be a home for life. It provided them with the opportunity to be homeowners, investors and to satisfy their aspirations. As a councillor I fought very hard to get Right to Buy in. It's very bad now that people are being shortchanged and their aspirations shattered,' Eckersley told me. He feels that the battle to pay residents such paltry sums for their properties amounts to an abuse of power by a public authority. 'It seems the council instead of acting as responsible public authority, is behaving more aggressively than the worst sort of commercial developer,' he told me. Tribal loyalties die hard and he still considers himself a Tory, but with growing reservations. 'I'm rather losing touch with the Tory establishment – I'm probably seen as a disrupter now. There are a mixture of property rights and human rights which are being interfered with,' he said. What has particularly upset him is the way that the government refers to places like the Aylesbury as 'sink estates', which is 'frankly disrespectful, particularly on those estates where a fifth to a quarter of residents are leaseholders'.

Toby has a personal reason to feel empathy with Beverley and the other homeowners because Southwark Council had planned to demolish his own home back in the 1970s as part of its slum clearance programme. Then as now, Southwark Council was a cheerleader for demolition, with one former resident recalling the council adopting the slogan 'let's rebuild it end to end'. Toby remembers how even the now highly sought-after Georgian squares and terraces of Kennington Park Road and Addington Square came within the 'red line' which signified demolition. His own Victorian cottage, tucked between Kennington and the Elephant and Castle, was earmarked for the wrecking ball as part of the wholesale clearance, but he successfully fought the Compulsory Purchase Order, taking the case all the way to the Court of Appeal and winning. His anger at a socialist administration trying to take his property away from him was one reason he joined the Conservatives, but now with a Conservative government supporting estate regeneration by both Labour and Conservative councils, he feels the small property owner has been betrayed. 'The corporate steamroller seems to me to be taking precedence over the protection of individual rights and property rights. I think it's going to come back and bite them,' he said.

'SINK ESTATES'

In other parts of Europe, very similar public housing schemes have worked well and continue to function as their architects intended. But in Britain, large-scale housing projects, built according to modernist and socialist principles, collided directly with the individualistic and neoliberal political and economic culture that became embedded from the 1980s. Aspects of New Labour policy attempted a 'third way', putting housing associations in charge in place of councils, but this failed to turn the tide, and indeed critics claim that instead it significantly ramped up the privatization agenda. Today, the result is the determination, openly admitted by many in government, to get rid of social housing altogether, for all but a tiny minority. In recent years there has been a revival of interest in the Brutalist architectural style which characterizes many postwar estates and those that are listed – and therefore safe from demolition – such as Erno Goldfinger's Trellick and Balfron Towers and Lubetkin's Hallfield Estate – are very popular with social housing and private sector residents. Nevertheless, the association between postwar estates and deprivation is strong and is reflected by the frequent references politicians and media make to 'Sink Estates'.

As with so much that happens in this country, the roots of what was to come for housing were not just down to Mrs Thatcher. It had all started a decade or so before, in the US – both in terms of policy and myth-making, which has played a large part in creating the 'sink estate' narrative. In 1972, an American architect, Oscar Newman, published a book called *Defensible Space: People and Design in the Violent City*, based on a study of crime in three New York housing 'projects' – the term for public housing in the US. The core of his argument was that crime was rife in housing projects, but that it need not be seen as the result of social problems but opportunism and could therefore be dealt with through design. His conclusion was that the modernist design of housing estates and tower blocks in particular produced crime (Manhattan skyscrapers notwithstanding). They should be knocked down and replaced with low-rise housing where private territory and boundaries could be marked out and defended, giving individuals a sense of ownership and deterring criminals from entering. Conveniently, this was also a far simpler and cheaper solution than addressing the structural economic causes of deprivation. His ideas coincided with decisions by American policymakers to introduce housing vouchers, rental subsidies similar to housing benefit, subsidizing people to move out of the projects to private rented housing elsewhere – another policy that the UK was to adopt a decade later.

Newman's views about defensible space and individual

responsibility chimed with an increasingly individualistic and neo-liberal political culture and spread like wildfire through American policy circles, where he became the man of the moment. The demolition of one of the largest housing projects in the US, Pruitt–Igoe in Missouri, in 1972, was televised in the US and became a national symbol of his approach. It eerily foreshadows today's demolition agenda and provides a context for it. A couple of years later, Newman was invited by the BBC to visit the Aylesbury Estate to make a documentary about his ideas for the influential *Horizon* series. The film intercuts the demolition of Pruitt–Igoe with dimly lit stairwells on the Aylesbury. 'One wonders, what happens to the children who grow up here? Do they ever really feel any sense of pride,' intoned Newman as he walked around. 'One wonders, will these children grow up to become the criminals that we seem to have so much of in America,' he continued, despite the fact that crime rates on the Aylesbury were low and bore no resemblance to those of the US housing projects Newman had been studying. After the broadcast the architecture magazine *Building Design* claimed that the estate had been 'scarred forever by Oscar Newman's trial by TV'.[17]

Heavily promoted by geographer Alice Coleman, who became Margaret Thatcher's adviser, Newman's ideas on defensible space took off in the UK in the 1980s[18] and led to a police-backed design policy, Secured by Design, which has ensured that defensible space, and the high security it brings, has become a condition of planning permission on all new development in the UK, in particular for housing, schools and public buildings. The consequence is that Newman's emphasis on territory and individual ownership, which does not sit easily with communal public housing, is now reflected in high-security housing estates where gates, grilles and forbidding high fences have become the norm.

Secured by Design guidelines also state that security must be higher in high crime areas – which correlate with poverty – with the result that deprived parts of Britain are taking on an almost militarized atmosphere which feels alienating and intimidating.[19] For example, a housing development I visited in East London, which was the winner of a Secured by Design National Award, had small windows, reinforced steel doors with full-size iron gates in front and a grey aluminium roof. Because the rise of defensible space has paralleled the marginalization of social housing, there are now estates which are heavily 'defended' places with high concentrations of poverty and unemployment which do seem to feed directly into the 'sink estate' narrative. Work by the consultancy Space Syntax, which found that housing estates were close to areas where the 2011 London riots took place, has also influenced politicians keen to demolish estates.[20]

For politicians the Aylesbury has been the emblematic 'sink estate' virtually since it opened in 1970, even if many of its residents don't see it that way. But most important of all has been the role of myth-making in creating this narrative which began with Newman and sheds light on the story of decline in public housing more widely around the UK. As far as the British public were concerned the Aylesbury really shot to fame as the poster child for urban deprivation when newly elected Tony Blair stood in the middle of it and talked of 'estates where the biggest employer is the drugs industry, where all that is left of the high hopes of the postwar planners is derelict concrete'. Since then journalists have referred to the Aylesbury variously as 'the estate from hell',[21] and 'hell's waiting room',[22] despite its low crime figures. The most extreme example comes from Channel 4, which brought the dismal picture of a sink estate to daily audiences of millions. Since 2004, Channel 4's long running 'ident' – identity logo – has been taken from the Aylesbury, with grainy black and white footage shown panning across rubbish-strewn balconies, while the concrete structures shift into place to form the Channel 4 logo; except that, unbeknown to viewers, the washing lines, shopping trolleys, rubbish bags and satellite dishes were never really there[23] – they were added in as props by the film makers to make it look as dystopian as possible. While most people watching wouldn't know the images of decay are from the Aylesbury, the local community certainly does.

THE 'RENT GAP': FROM SOCIAL HOUSING TO SUPER PRIME

> I've put the bulldozing of sink estates at the heart of turn-around Britain.
>
> David Cameron, *Sunday Times*, 10 January 2016

In this piece in the *Sunday Times*, which launched the former prime minister's 'Sink Estates' initiative, Cameron stuck carefully to the by now familiar story of estate failure:

> There is one issue that . . . for me, epitomises both the scale of the challenge we face and the nature of state failure over decades. It's our housing estates . . . step outside in the worst estates, and you're confronted by concrete slabs dropped from on high, brutal high rise towers and dark alleyways that are a gift to criminals and drug dealers. The police often talk about the importance of designing out crime, but these estates actually designed it in.

While this line of argument was familiar to some, the really interesting part of Cameron's piece came next:

> There's a second critical by-product of our plan. Tomorrow a report from Savills will show that this kind of programme could help to catalyse the building of hundreds of thousands of new homes in London alone. This is because existing estates were built at a lower density than many modern developments – poorly laid-out, with wasted open space that was neither park nor garden. So regeneration will work best in areas where land values are high, because new private homes, built attractively and at a higher density, will fund the regeneration of the rest of the estate.[. . .]
>
> I believe that together we can tear down anything that stands in our way.

As part of the initiative he announced a proposal to transform a hundred estates, publish an Estates Regeneration Strategy and establish an advisory panel chaired by Tory grandee Lord Heseltine. As with so many significant changes in the direction of government policy, the ground had already been prepared with a pamphlet published by the Conservative think tank Policy Exchange, together with a consultancy called Create Streets, which suggested that high-rise estates should be replaced with streets. It came out in 2013, shortly before its co-author, Alex Morton, went on to become housing adviser in Downing Street, where he oversaw the passage of the controversial Housing and Planning Act 2016 into law. The Savills report which Cameron referred to, 'City of Villages: More Homes, Better Communities' – in fact published by the New Labour think tank IPPR – includes an analysis by estate agents Savills and was edited by Lord Adonis, the former Labour cabinet minister who was appointed by the Conservatives as chair of the National Infrastructure Commission. Adonis was blunt about the motives behind the report. 'The scale of council-owned land is vast and greatly under-appreciated,' he told the *Financial Times*. 'There are particularly large concentrations of council-owned land in inner London and this is some of the highest-priced land in the world ... [The] local authority planning regime has got to adapt properly to the potential for [market-priced rent] developments.'[24]

A key point Adonis makes is that although people have bought their own homes that does not affect the council's right to demolish. 'It is important to understand that local authority development rights are unaffected by thirty years of "Right to Buy", which has transferred leaseholds but not freeholds. They do not therefore undermine the power of local authorities – or housing associations ... – to redevelop estates,' the report states. In London 50 per cent of all property is leasehold, so according to this logic half of all homeowners in London could at one fell swoop have their property rights removed – although fortunately for the majority of them, their landlord is not a local authority or housing association. Of the 3,500 estates in London, housing hundreds of thousands of people, even now only a small percentage has been redeveloped. Adonis writes in the report: 'London's few dozen estate regeneration schemes of recent years have focused particularly on notorious "sink estates"' – a claim disputed by many residents. In words to strike fear into the heart of any council resident anywhere in London, he continues: 'The challenge is to extend the creation of new city villages well beyond such doomed estates. Borough by borough, a city village programme, centred on systematic estate regeneration, is required.' So it is clear that if these plans are even partially realized they will completely alter the social make-up of London.

This policy – of redeveloping estates – is driven by American academic Neil Smith's concept of the 'rent gap', which he developed as a different way of looking at gentrification. The model favoured since the 1970s maintained that the middle classes moved back to the post-industrial city attracted by new economic opportunities and lifestyle as the former spaces of industry opened themselves up to trendy loft living. Smith looks at the gap between the rent a property currently earns and what it could earn if redeveloped for new inhabitants. He argues that when that gap becomes big enough, developers become interested and private capital flows in, attracted by the potential to make large profits.[25] Academics have claimed that the failure to maintain estates, which keeps prices low, contributes to a 'state-induced rent gap'.[26] When he talks of local authorities adapting to the 'potential' for market-priced development, Adonis himself is clear that the 'rent gap' offered by potentially very high land values is driving estate regeneration. He argues that at a time of acute housing crisis, redevelopment is the only way to build the numbers of houses required, as the sales of new expensive homes also help pay for new affordable homes. Again, this viewpoint frames the housing crisis as being caused by a lack of supply alone, which it is not. Building large numbers of luxury apartments at the expense of poorer people is not helping.

The demolition and rebuild approach isn't just down to the high land values estates sit on, however. It also comes back to tax. A key incentive for developers and local authorities to pursue demolition over refurbishment is the fact that new-build homes are exempt from the 20 per cent VAT that refurbishment is subject to. Estate demolition has already made its mark on London. It is the consensus among nearly everyone in what is known as the 'housing industry', from the numerous local authorities who have commissioned Savills to undertake research for them, to developers, housing associations and consultants. Despite the tide of local opposition each scheme unleashes, the fact is that councils, who are fully behind this approach, possess the land and can drive the policy forward. It is rapidly becoming the standard orthodoxy. In this it is likely to be enormously helped by new provisions in the Housing and Planning Act granting automatic 'planning permission in principle' to brownfield sites, which include housing estates, allowing councils to bypass the consultation process with residents living there. Instead, the National Infrastructure Commission will be the body ultimately in charge of housing, and that is headed up by Lord Adonis himself. The victory of the Aylesbury residents at the public inquiry is therefore remarkable and very important in offering residents and campaigners a way to oppose redevelopment. But it is also notable that the decision to block the Compulsory Purchase Order was based on how the residents were treated by the council, rather than opposition to the redevelopment. The inspector and the secretary of state both accepted that the scheme would benefit the area if it were allowed to go ahead.

After the Aylesbury decision campaigners hoped the tide was turning against demolition, but Chris Brown, who describes himself as an 'ethical developer' and is against estate regeneration programmes of this type, believes that little has changed, although the ideological zeal of the Downing Street advisers who initially pushed forward on this has been replaced by a less aggressive approach. 'There was a genuine attempt to destroy council housing estates in London,' he told me, but 'it's essentially business as usual but on slightly better behaviour, which is a huge disappointment'. Similarly, hopes that the new Labour Mayor of London, Sadiq Khan, would stick to his manifesto commitment that estate regeneration would take place only with residents' support were dashed when his draft good practice guide on the subject failed to include this requirement and actively discouraged giving tenants a vote, claiming there is 'a potential reason for caution around using ballots or votes, since they risk turning a complex set of issues that affects different people in different ways over many years into a simple yes/no decision'.[27]

Because of the role played by central and local government in estate regeneration, for many academics the population shifts which result from it are no longer known as 'gentrification', but 'state-led gentrification'. For those at the sharp end, even this change in terminology fails to define it; at an event I attended on the housing crisis in 2016, one member of the audience after another got up to say that the term 'gentrification' no longer covered what was happening: 'It's the wrong terminology for a state-sponsored demolition programme,' one said. 'It's a positive term for some people which doesn't describe what is really happening,' said another. For academic and activist Bob Catterall, it's 'domicide'.

DEMOCRATIC FAILURE

While the Heygate and the Aylesbury were successfully labelled as 'sink estates' – albeit that many of their residents didn't see it like that – it is impossible to describe Cressingham Gardens in Lambeth this way. Built alongside the rolling landscape of South London's Brockwell Park, with its views over London, the estate was described by a past president of the Royal Institution of British Architects as 'warm and informal ... one of the nicest small schemes in England'.[28] SAVE Britain's Heritage said it was of 'special architectural and historic interest' and hailed it as 'a remarkable example of a model village layout designed with great imagination and care to provide attractive community living'.[29] It is also a great example of the rent gap, sitting as it does on very high land values, with apartments on Brockwell Gate, the neighbouring newly built gated development, selling for £650,000 at the time of writing. Unsurprisingly, residents love living on Cressingham Gardens, although they also complain that repairs and maintenance have been consistently neglected by the council. Even so, 81 per cent opposed Lambeth Council's planned demolition. Once again, the by-now familiar story of democratic failure is playing out here.

In 2013 Lambeth Council put forward several options for consultation with residents, ranging from refurbishment, building new homes alongside refurbishment to partial demolition, full demolition and rebuilding. Groups were set up to consider the various scenarios and Social Life, a consultancy which specializes in community participation in design, was appointed as part of Lambeth's commitment to being a 'Co-operative Council'. But before the groups had completed their reports, residents were informed that the refurbishment options would not be consulted on further because they were too expensive. Residents, architects and consultants appointed by the council were left aghast at Lambeth's treatment of residents and its 'co-operative' concept. Commitment to consultation rang very hollow in the context of Social Life's research, which concluded that 'the vast majority of residents would prefer to stay on the estate'.[30]

The residents were forbidden by the council to hold meetings in the estate's community hall, but despite this a very strong campaign built up in 2015. They took the council's decision to demolish the estate to the High Court, which ruled that a judicial review could be submitted to challenge the decision to 'abruptly close down' consultation on options which were strongly supported by residents.[31] To their surprise and relief, the residents, represented by human rights lawyers Leigh Day, won on the basis that the consultation was unlawful, and the council was ordered to consult again, on refurbishment – including a community-developed 'People's Plan'. But all that happened is that a few months later the council voted its plan through again, claiming that all the refurbishment options were unaffordable owing to government cuts and constraints on the council's Housing Revenue Account. Residents then worked tirelessly around the clock and built up a new case, questioning the council's financial calculations and claiming that the 'People's Plan' was misrepresented. They were granted another judicial review, which they lost. At the time of writing they had applied for permission to appeal, while also considering bringing forward a leaseholder action around the council's failure to maintain their homes. If all these avenues fail, they will then fight compulsory purchase, like the Aylesbury homeowners are doing, so the whole process will involve more lengthy court proceedings and take years. Because councils hire hugely expensive lawyers in these cases, sagas like this cost vast amounts of money which could instead be spent on essential public services, including housing.

Although councils have a statutory obligation to consult local residents about proposed new development, accusations of sham consultations, derided as a tick-box exercise, are not limited to Cressingham Gardens. In Southwark, the lobbying company Four Communications has worked with developers to provide the required 'Statement of Community Involvement' – meaning community consultation – on no fewer than ten developments in Elephant and Castle, none of which include any social housing. According to campaign group Better Elephant, just thirteen people were consulted about luxury residential tower block Strata Tower.[32]

This lack of real democratic accountability has long been apparent in the private public partnerships which have characterized housing throughout the UK over the last twenty years. Many stock transfer ballots – where tenants are asked to vote on whether they wish to transfer their homes from council to housing association control – were carried out amid accusations of ballot rigging in local authorities around the country. Wrong-footing opponents by holding ballots early was a favoured tactic. For example, a parliamentary select committee heard how Islington gave one day's notice of a ballot in 2004. Obstruction and intimidation of opposition campaigns were also commonplace.[33] Other examples include holding consultations during holiday periods and dirty tricks used in the forced evictions resulting from New Labour's Housing Market Renewal Initiative, a programme which ran between 2002 and 2011. The Scottish government's handling of planning permission for US President Donald Trump's golf course in Aberdeenshire was also widely questioned: although Aberdeenshire Council rejected the application in 2007, former Scottish First Minister Alex Salmond took the unprecedented decision to 'call in' the application, which was subsequently given planning permission. This set Trump on a collision course with local residents living in properties near the course, which he wished to acquire and demolish.[34] The bullying, intimidation and harassment faced by residents have been documented in the acclaimed film *You've Been Trumped*, which reveals how residents' water and electricity were cut off and tonnes of earth piled up next to their homes.[35]

Today, it feels like this failure of democratic representation for local communities, and the dirty tricks that go with it, is becoming standard practice. In a House of Commons debate in 2013, Labour MP Thomas Docherty, a former lobbyist, shared with Parliament some of the techniques of his former colleagues, recounting stories of lobbyists being planted in public meetings to heckle people who opposed their clients' schemes. His stories chime with a wealth of anecdotal evidence of dirty tricks, including fake letter-writing campaigns and even actors attending planning meetings. Martyn, a film maker from Brighton, described to me how he had been offered 'cash in brown envelopes' to attend a planning meeting and pose as a supporter of Frank Gehry's controversial plans for an iconic new development of 750 luxury apartments on the seafront. He remembers how 'at least five of us' from the drama school where he was studying were approached by an events company and asked if they'd like to participate. 'We were told to go there and shout down the local opposition to the development. A couple of people were pointed out to us – residents, leaders of the local opposition – and we were told to be louder than them and be positive about the development. We were paid on exit, cash in hand, I think it was £50 or £100. I was there and I'm not proud of it. It is something that horrifies me,' he said.[36] In Parliament, Docherty described dirty tricks as 'utterly unacceptable', although 'not a crime'.[37] It is this flouting of the spirit of the law while keeping to the letter of the law which, like tax evasion and 'financial viability assessments', seems to characterize so much of political culture today. This sort of behaviour is not on the whole illegal but it avoids making any contribution to society and at times spills over into corruption.

One of the most blatant examples I've come across of the intimidation that can accompany consultation processes is the admission by a lobbying company called Westbourne of methods whereby 'we shit them up' in order 'to scare the living daylights out of people'.[38] In this particular case, Westbourne was explaining to a closed seminar how the company had worked to quell local opposition to argue the case in favour of building HS2, the high-speed rail link. The lobbyist giving the presentation revealed the technique they used was to create compelling stories to change the parameters of the debate, by inventing a framework which set wealthy residents in the Chilterns – 'posh NIMBYs' – against working-class people. The strategy was 'posh people standing in the way of working-class people getting jobs', with posters for the campaign asking people to choose between 'their lawns or our jobs'. A planning academic who attended the Westbourne seminar told me afterwards: 'It was very coldly targeted and very strategic in the way that images were put forward. That's the way PR works, but it was so calculating. I came away thinking this has implications for the way democratic debate develops in this country.'

This 'class war' narrative is also favoured by local councils in London, with Lambeth pitting leaseholders against tenants and arguing in court that the campaign to save Cressingham Gardens was unrepresentative and driven by the interests of NIMBY home-owners.[39] The same class struggle story was wheeled out again in an attempt to defend Lambeth's hugely contentious library closure programme which plans to turn libraries into gyms, alongside unstaffed books sections. Labour Councillor Matthew Bennett – in fact the cabinet member for housing – tweeted in response to the occupation of Lambeth's Carnegie Library: 'While they knock back wine in the library, almost 5,000 homeless Lambeth children go to bed in temporary accommodation,' in a much mocked attempt to claim that library cutbacks would hit the middle classes and that the money spent on libraries would be better used to improve housing for working-class tenants. Local people and even fellow Labour councillors were not impressed with the attempt to shift the blame for housing cuts on to the library protesters. Critics on social media accused Bennett of 'ridiculous doublespeak' and queried 'when those children get up, where will they go to make a future for themselves? Not to the libraries you're closing.' After questioning the council's policy towards estate demolition and library closures, Labour Councillor Rachel Heywood was suspended from Lambeth Labour for six months.

In this topsy-turvy world where cash-strapped councils spend vast sums on legal battles with residents and sell prime land for a fraction of its value, the councils' argument is that, starved of funds and facing unprecedented cuts, estate regeneration is the only way they can build new housing. Lambeth also claim they are building new council homes through their controversial housing company. But the numbers are minimal; on Cressingham Gardens the net gain in homes for social rent after the estate has been demolished and rebuilt would be just twenty-seven.

It is true that councils are facing a perfect storm of cuts and austerity. But demolition and rebuild is not the answer, and forcing it through not only means eroding local democracy but stands in the way of the need to look at the housing crisis holistically. This is an issue which brings together the influx of global capital with failures in the land and planning system and failures in the benefits system, and cannot be solved simply by building new homes. It also means other ways out of this bind are not considered. The zeal with which so many councils are embracing the demolition and rebuild agenda means a rapid reshaping of London is underway. Although the Conservatives are every bit as keen on estate regeneration, I have focused in this chapter on Lambeth and Southwark. These are Labour councils dominated by Progress, the faction on the right of the Labour Party, and there is no doubt that many of their members believe that the market mechanisms and private financing behind the current approach to increasing private renting and home ownership are the best way – perhaps the only way – of providing public goods such as housing. Proof that there are other ways of delivering significant amounts of housing which work with existing communities, rather than demolishing them, will be looked at in chapter 6.

However, even if the 'TINA' argument were taken at face value – Margaret Thatcher's famous mantra, 'There is No Alternative' – there is an undercurrent in play which taps directly into claims from residents that deliberate social cleansing is also a policy aim. Aditya Chakrabortty is the *Guardian*'s senior economics commentator and spent six months investigating the demolition and rebuilding of the Woodberry Down Estate in North London.[40] He told me how, during the course of the investigation someone from the council suggested to him that they should speak off the record – which usually implies that there is important, perhaps confidential, information to impart. The council official explained to Aditya, 'the thing is, what we find on council estates, a lot of people who live on them, they suffer from obesity and a lot of them are benefit claimants, or on drugs, or worse'. There is a symbiotic relationship between the deliberate attempts of state-led gentrification to increase land and property prices – with the consequent change in social composition of the area – and a casual, everyday discrimination against people on low incomes. This is reflected in popular culture with the emergence of reality TV programmes such as Channel 5's *Can't Pay? We'll Take It Away!*, which shows bailiffs evicting people from their homes. Akin to racism, it is part of a much broader response to – and internal justification for – rapidly rising inequality in every sphere of our lives, described by a friend of mine from a deprived background as 'a crypto culture of hatred for the poor'. After the EU referendum he felt this came out into the open, with calls for 'idiots', 'plebs' and the 'uneducated' not to be allowed to vote.

4
From Bricks to Benefits

EXPULSIONS

In the summer of 2013, Jasmine was a nineteen-year-old single mum of an eleven-month-old baby living at Focus E15, a hostel in East London with a mother and baby unit. When Newham Council cut the funding for the hostel, Jasmine was told she was one of twenty-nine mothers who would be evicted. The council gave her a list of places to phone which they said might accept people on benefits, but she couldn't find anywhere. Her mother, Janice, remembers: 'We were literally phoning and phoning, so much so that Jasmine ended up with such a high phone bill she couldn't pay it.' The council told her that if she didn't find somewhere by the time she was evicted she would be moved to Hastings, Manchester or Birmingham, away from her mum, extended family and the support networks so essential to a mother of a new baby. 'I watched Jasmine getting really down and upset and she's got a history of vulnerability. I told her, "You've got to go out there and talk to the other mums,"' Janice said.

Eighteen-year old Sam, who was eight months pregnant at the time, lived just above Jasmine. 'I could see Jasmine's door from my window. We ended up talking and talking for ten hours flat,' she said. They explained that the mothers hadn't been encouraged to mix or talk to each other, but galvanized by what they were faced with they decided to draw up a petition and get a protest going. 'It was crap, but it worked. It literally said, "Sign here if you support us and you don't think we should be evicted,"' Sam said. The mums, three of whom were heavily pregnant, took to Stratford Broadway with their babies

Abigail lives with her two children in one room in Boundary House in Welwyn Garden City after she was moved out of London by Waltham Forest Borough Council. Her baby is seriously ill, which means she has to make regular hospital visits to London.

in their buggies and went to collect signatures for their handwritten petition. 'We were on Stratford Broadway and we saw these people with a stall shouting about the "bedroom tax". We pulled one of them over and asked them, "How do you get such a good petition together – how can we do ours better?"' Sam remembers.

Today Jasmine and Sam are among the most articulate housing campaigners in London, after their random encounter with an obscure left splinter group – best known for its 1980s anti-apartheid protest outside the South African embassy – helped the campaign to take off where others don't.[1] The unlikely coming together of these two groups provided resources and organizational know-how for the mums; the petition was typed, a Facebook page was set up, press were invited and suddenly the story, which combined babies and homelessness and was therefore a gift to the media, took off. 'We put together a press statement and we made the front page of the *Newham Recorder*,' Jasmine said. Emboldened by the media coverage but no further forward, the mums asked for a meeting with the mayor of Newham, Sir Robin Wales.

> We walked in [to the mayor's office] . . . and by then we'd done a few street stalls and had made the *Newham Recorder*, but what we'd said was just about our hostel, it wasn't about anything to do with the Council. The Mayor saw us and I introduced who we were and he said 'I think it's disgusting what you're doing' . . . and he's our Labour Mayor. And we was completely shocked and at that point we was still quite weak, we were a bit shaken up by him, when we got out of the meeting we were actually in tears, cuddling each other, 'he's our Mayor', one of the mums told academic Paul Watt.[2]

Sam said the mayor simply told them: 'If you can't afford to live in Newham, you can't afford to live in Newham.'

But despite their initial shock, the mayor's reaction spurred them on and they proceeded to organize a series of high-profile and successful actions, including the temporary occupation of a show flat in the former Olympic Village, where they held a children's party. They wanted to highlight the alleged housing 'legacy' of the London Olympics – which pledged to benefit local residents, notwithstanding that a one-bedroom flat in the area is more than £1,600 a month to rent, and thus far out of reach of most local people. This was followed by a two-week occupation of an empty and boarded-up block of flats on the Carpenters Estate, subject to similar contentious estate regeneration proposals as those going on in Southwark and Lambeth. The huge success of the Carpenters Estate occupation, with widespread media coverage and the involvement of comedian Russell Brand, saw the council backtrack on the eviction of the mums. Robin Wales was forced to issue a qualified apology, writing in the *Guardian* that 'although the decision was the right one, the way . . . the council initially dealt with the foyer families was unacceptable, and for that I apologise'.[3] All the twenty-nine mums were rehoused in Newham, but Robin Wales clearly hadn't forgiven them; he lost his temper and had to be physically restrained when they protested at the mayor's summer show, an incident which was filmed and has had tens of thousands of hits on YouTube, showing a red-faced Robin Wales being held back while shouting at Jasmine.[4] Following its investigation of a complaint, the council's standards advisory council found that Wales had breached the council's code of conduct by not treating a member of the public with respect.[5]

Since the campaign began, Focus E15 has gone from strength to strength: its members man their weekly stall, support new campaigns and speak at events across London and abroad. This experience has enabled some of them to find their voice in a way they hadn't before. Jasmine has spoken to a housing rally of 50,000 people and has been to Italy with European housing activists. Another Focus E15 mum, Elina Garrick, who obtained a diploma from Birkbeck College, said: 'I couldn't go to university because of my children but this is my university.' And Sam, who has never been abroad before, has been invited to talk about housing in Budapest with Jasmine. They have spawned a number of plays, won the Ron Todd/ Inspiring Young People Award[6] and received funding from the Network for Social Change, which means they now have an office in Stratford, named 'Sylvia's Corner' after the campaigner for women's suffrage Sylvia Pankhurst. Yet, for all their success, the issue they managed to highlight, that councils are forcibly exporting families out of London to other cities, has got far, far worse and what was seen as exceptional in 2013 is now the norm. As for Robin Wales, discussing the changing social demographics of the area at a conference recently, he told his audience that: 'The middle classes are swarming into our borough at a rate of knots.'[7]

THE DOMINO EFFECT OF EXPORTING HOMELESSNESS AROUND THE COUNTRY

Twenty-two-year-old Lillie, who has a two-and-a-half-year-old daughter called Maisie, became homeless in 2016 and was rehoused by Waltham Forest Borough Council outside London, in Boundary House, on the outskirts of Welwyn Garden City. The block of one-room flats of temporary accommodation, which has no lift, was once student accommodation for nurses and was never intended for families. From there it is a long and expensive commute back to Walthamstow, in north-east London, where most of Boundary House's new residents are from. There are no shops nearby, it takes half an hour to get to the nearest GP and the train fare to London is £18.50, not including £4.80 for a single bus fare or £3.50 for a cab to the station. The residents live with mould, damp and cockroach infestations, and some of the mums sleep three or four to a room; Elina Garrick was rehoused by Newham Council in one room in Boundary House for two years with her three children, who are three, five and eight, before the council offered her a home in Basildon in Essex, which is even further away from central London. It was not what she wanted and she would have liked to fight with the support of Focus E15 for a better home, but she was unable to continue to live in the squalid conditions, as the mould in their room made her daughter sick with frequent respiratory illnesses.

I met Elina, Lillie, her parents, Tim and Julie, and other Boundary House residents at the Waltham Forest Council housing offices in 2016 when they had finally managed to get a meeting with John Knight, Waltham Forest's assistant director of housing. Tim explained to me how difficult it was for the family since Lillie had been moved:

'We were hoping, because Lillie's got certain issues, that she could be in this area so we could support her. They've sent her to Welwyn Garden City and we can't get there because the train fare is so expensive.' As for Lillie's boyfriend, Maisie's dad, he works in Leyton and is living with his own mother to help her with her rent, because although she is working as well, she doesn't earn enough to pay it all. With Lillie's partner only able to visit, it has been difficult for them to keep their relationship going, although they have managed. Julie explained that the family's housing problems don't stop there, with her two other children at home and her other married daughter also homeless and dividing her time between her mum's house and her in-laws. 'I'm having a nightmare,' Julie said. 'I asked, "Why can't I give my house to my kids", but they won't let me do that. They'd rather put them miles away, isolated, where there's not even a shop.' Recently Lillie had her benefit sanctioned because she couldn't get to the benefit office in Walthamstow on time, and as a result she only receives £40 a week. Abigail, another resident, has been housed in one room with her three-year-old daughter and six-month-old baby, whose serious medical condition requires frequent visits to hospital in London.

At the meeting with John Knight it was quickly made clear that despite their hopes, Waltham Forest Borough Council was not prepared to review its decision to house local residents at Boundary House, which Knight claimed 'meets our requirements', although even Newham Council pledged in 2016 to no longer house people there. 'Unfortunately we don't have access to enough accommodation to house residents locally,' Knight said. The rest of the meeting was taken up with one tenant after another describing the damp, mould and cockroach infestations they were experiencing, which Knight saw in legalistic terms as 'a conflict of information between what Yasmin [his deputy] has reported to me and what you are saying'.

Boundary House is run by Theori Housing Management Ltd, a private sector company which according to its website provides 'effective property maintenance and responsive repair services'. The website goes on to describe Theori as 'specialists in the property sector with a property portfolio, in excess of £500 million and growing on a weekly basis'.[8] When the discussion turned to the issue of overcrowding,

Knight again resorted to a legalistic view, referring to the 'technical definition' of statutory overcrowding which counts children up to one year as zero and up to ten as half a person. When asked what was the maximum amount of time someone could expect to be in temporary accommodation, he responded: 'You are nowhere near the people who've been in temporary accommodation the longest – we have people in temporary accommodation who have been there for ten years.'

The discussion moved on to the 'bidding system' for social housing, as many councils use a 'choice-based lettings system', designed to give 'customers' more 'choice' about where they live. The Labour government hoped to persuade most authorities to move to this system by 2010, claiming it would allow people to make their own choices and make the system more open about what housing is allocated to whom, with ads that people can bid for placed online. But with so little social housing available and an absurdly complicated points system to navigate, none of the 'customers' at the meeting seemed to have any choices at all. Rahmo, who shares a double bed with her two kids, aged seven and four, is a smartly dressed young woman who has lived in Boundary House for three years. Although she has a job in a care home, she is able to work only at weekends when she brings her children up to London and gets help with childcare from her family. 'I can't have a boyfriend, I have no privacy, I can only work at the weekends when I can have my kids looked after – it's really tough. I keep coming here [the Waltham Forest housing office] and they say "keep on bidding". I didn't get anywhere so I didn't bid for a month and they closed my account,' she told me.

As social housing becomes a relic from the past, more and more people on housing benefit are being housed in the private rented sector, with over a third of all tenants on benefit in the UK renting privately in 2016.[9] In London, 27 per cent of all households rent privately, significantly more than live in social housing,[10] and Shelter has estimated that by 2025 the figure will be 41 per cent.[11] The think tank London's Poverty Profile estimates that there are 860,000 people living in poverty in the private rented sector, which is more than in any other tenure – a figure which includes over a quarter of a million children[12] – and that of those claiming housing benefit, more than half are in work.[13] People are being pushed into poverty. In the past housing benefit covered the rent for those who couldn't afford to pay because they were out of work or on low incomes. That is no longer the case. Today housing benefit is calculated according to a fiendishly complicated market-based formula called Local Housing Allowance. Introduced in 2008, that allowance is now often too low to cover rising rents and so people are being moved out of London – and other 'higher value' places around the country. From the moment it came in, it was clear that Local Housing Allowance would not meet private rent costs for everybody in their entirety, which was a significant issue,[14] but the gap between rents and housing benefit became far bigger after housing benefit was cut in 2011. At the same time, while rents continue to rise, wages have registered a fall of more than 25 per cent in real terms since the financial crisis. This means people in work but eligible for housing benefit are particularly hard hit, with the UK suffering the biggest drop in wages of any of the thirty-five OECD countries except the Czech Republic, Estonia and Latvia.[15]

The irony is that the Coalition government's rationale for reforming Local Housing Allowance was that cutting the amount paid to private landlords would help bring rents down – and therefore reduce the housing benefit bill; the government made it plain that it expected private landlords to reduce rents as a result of the reforms. 'What we have seen so far, as housing benefit has been reformed and reduced, is that rent levels have come down, so we have stopped ripping off the taxpayer,' then Prime Minister David Cameron told Parliament in 2012.[16] The idea was that Local Housing Allowance would pay for the lowest thirtieth percentile of rents – reduced from the fiftieth – meaning that theoretically the cheapest 30 per cent of rental properties in an area should be available to tenants on benefit. But, rather than coming down, rents across the board in London – and other parts of the country – have gone up. There are very few properties at all in London affordable to people on Local Housing Allowance. In Newham in 2016, LHA was capped at £788 per month for a one-bedroom flat. The average rent for a one-bed flat was £966 per month, leaving a shortfall of £178 for renters on benefit to fill.[17] Lillie described her attempts to find a place and said she had enquired about countless properties but found nothing she could remotely afford which corresponded to the Local Housing Allowance rate. 'I've even rang studio flats and been told they're going for £995,' she said, to which Knight replied: 'Very frankly, these flats are not advertised for mothers with children.'

Pressed on this, Knight conceded that Local Housing Allowance caters for 'a niche market' which did not seem to be providing housing in the cheapest 30 per cent of private rented properties in Waltham Forest, despite the guidance from the Department of Work and Pensions that it should. In Newham, according to Freedom of Information requests made by the *Newham Recorder*, the consequence is that more than 540 households have been moved out of the borough between 2012 and 2015, with some ending up in Birmingham and Leeds and one family going as far as Middlesbrough.[18] Newham's tenfold increase in the number of homeless families exported out of London between 2012 and 2015 is a London-wide trend. Figures leaked to the *Independent* from London Councils – the body representing the capital's thirty-two boroughs – revealed that close to 50,000 families have been moved out of their boroughs, and of these 6 per cent were moved out of London.[19] The number of children affected is likely to be in the hundreds of thousands. While the shortage of housing is obviously a factor, the main reason that the figures have soared is because the introduction of Local Housing Allowance came at the same time as changes in the law brought in under the Localism Act in 2012, giving local authorities the power to force families to accept the housing offered to them. The law means that, if they refuse, the council is discharged of its duty to house them, leaving them literally on the streets.

Families have no choice but to accept offers they don't want in places far away from home. This is creating a housing crisis in other cities such as Luton, where Westminster, Waltham Forest and Wandsworth all house families; this in turn means that Luton has nowhere to put its own residents, and exports them to Milton Keynes, Bedford, Northampton and Peterborough. This crazy situation is the consequence of making a dysfunctional market system the ultimate arbiter of housing for the poor. Councils in higher value areas receive more Local Housing Allowance for their residents. While that doesn't meet rents in their own borough it pays for housing in outlying areas, creating a domino effect around the country. Councillor Tom Shaw, from Luton Borough Council, explained: 'The Local Housing Allowance in Luton for a one-bedroom place will be around £650 and London local housing allowance is £760, so the landlord can get an extra £110 by doing a deal with a London borough.' But Luton also has a housing shortage so 'the stupid bit about it is we're having to do the same and move our people . . . so Luton people are further north and London people are moving north to Luton.'[20]

In 2015, Titina Nzolameso won a protracted legal battle in the Supreme Court, preventing Westminster Council from removing her family to Milton Keynes, in a judgment that was hailed as having a significant impact on how councils would carry out their statutory housing duty. Nzolameso, who has serious health problems, lived with her children in Westminster between 2008 and 2012 until the cap on Local Housing Allowance meant she could no longer afford the rent and her landlord evicted her. The council offered her a property in Milton Keynes which she rejected as it was too far away from her GP and because her children would have to change schools.[21] She appealed against the decision and lost, then appealed again in the Supreme Court, and during the ongoing legal process Westminster's children's services department refused to house the family together, placing the children in care. Arguing that under the provisions of the Housing Act 1996 all local housing authorities are required to secure accommodation within their own district 'so far as reasonably practicable', the Supreme Court ruled that Westminster had acted unlawfully because it failed to provide evidence that housing was not available closer to the borough.[22] Responding to the ruling, Nzolameso said: 'When I first refused the offer of accommodation in Milton Keynes, I never envisaged that my children would be taken away from me. There was an obligation on the council to offer me accommodation in the district which I applied to or closer to it. Westminster simply failed to lawfully address that question. Councils now can't just say: "We haven't got anywhere else available."'

And yet, despite the Supreme Court case, in 2017 Westminster

Council ruled that as part of its official Homelessness Policies 'many' of the offers of housing made to residents 'are likely to be outside London'. Research commissioned by the council concluded that Slough, Maidenhead, Leicester, Birmingham and Coventry 'presented the best opportunities', although even there the supply of suitable properties was found to be limited.[23] While Westminster may be the first council to make this official policy, many other local authorities use similar methods. Nathaniel Mathews, who is the senior solicitor at Hackney Community Law Centre, told me he was working on a case against Brent Council where the extended family look after the children so the mother can work, but the family has been repeatedly offered a property in the Midlands. 'I've no idea whether we'll win it or not. They'll say "we have no properties" and to some extent that's right. Westminster homes in East London, East London homes in Harrow, Barking and Dagenham, Grays in Essex,' he explained. As far as he's concerned the 'worst' councils are in central London: 'It's Westminster, Kensington and Chelsea, Hammersmith and Fulham.' Research by Kate Hardy from Leeds University Business School and Tom Gillespie at Sheffield University, undertaken with Focus E15, found that close to half the participants in their study in East London had been advised to leave the capital. 'People facing homelessness are often being informally or formally "advised" to move out of Newham, and 44 per cent had been offered or advised to consider moving out of London altogether. This puts incredible strains on families. It disproportionately affects single mothers, with serious implications for the well-being and life chances of their children,' Hardy said.[24]

Nathaniel Mathews describes what Westminster is doing as 'Lady Porter mark 2 via the backdoor', referring to the 1980s 'Homes for Votes' scandal when Westminster City Council leader and arch Thatcherite Dame Shirley Porter instigated a policy to change the social composition of marginal wards in the borough to ensure they were more likely to vote Conservative. The policy, called 'Building Stable Communities', saw the council put aside council homes to sell them, while moving students, nurses and homeless voters to poor condition housing elsewhere. In many ways the illegal decisions by Westminster

Council, which resulted in Lady Porter being forced to pay the council £12.3 million, are now standard practice across London. The only difference is that Lady Porter deliberately planned these outcomes, while today social cleansing is the result of crude market forces interacting with poorly thought-out policymaking – with disastrous consequences. As for the housing benefit bill, despite the huge cuts to a range of housing benefits, including Local Housing Allowance, which is frozen until 2020, housing benefit has gone up by over £7 billion in ten years, and is expected to be more than £24 billion in 2017.[25]

Yet whereas the bedroom tax, which will be looked at later in this chapter, has hit the headlines, the abject failure of Local Housing Allowance has slipped by almost unnoticed. This is partly because the Conservative government has presented it in terms of cuts to benefits welcome to their supporters and partly because the interaction between housing benefit and market forces is absurdly complicated and the tens of thousands of families displaced by the toxic combination of rising rents, falling wages and benefit cuts have so far been only a trickle in policy terms. Unfortunately, this is now becoming a steady stream, and with the government's further cuts to benefits it threatens to become a flood.

THE BANLIEUES

Westminster's Housing Options Service, which is what the homelessness office is now called, is behind the Edgware Road, at the end of a long street of pleasant-looking council blocks built by the London County Council in the 1930s. A quick look at Rightmove reveals that a two-bedroom flat in former local authority Orchardson House is now on the private rented market for £1,799 per month – £600 more than the maximum Local Housing Allowance for a two-bed flat in London. I was there because I wanted to see if what I'd heard about Westminster exporting families out of the borough would be borne out by the people waiting in the council's homeless office. It immediately was by Bouchra, the first woman I talked to, who was there with her two children, aged three and eleven months, and who was due to be evicted by their landlord the following day, after five years. This was her second visit so she knew she would be waiting all day and had brought food and toys for the children. On her previous visit she had been offered a flat in Uxbridge, but Bouchra, who is Moroccan, and her husband, who is Iraqi – although both are British citizens – didn't know where that was. She was given another chance and told she could come back the day before the bailiffs were due to evict them but to expect that anything they were offered 'would be far'. 'I don't want to go far away because I have no family and I'll have no friends, everyone I know is here,' she said. When I phoned her the next day she told me they'd been moved fourteen miles away to Barking, which would mean her husband would have to give up his job on the Edgware Road as he couldn't afford the commute.

I also met Bashir and Fayza, a softly spoken husband and wife from Eritrea. Both were homeless although Bashir worked at the BBC as a kitchen porter and Fayza was pregnant with their first child. Fayza was sleeping on the floor at a friend's house, which the friend was not happy about, and Bashir was sleeping on buses. When I asked him how often he did that, he said 'too much – sometimes every night'. He wasn't the only one either, telling me that when the driver shouts out the last stop there'll be two or three people asleep. The other person I spoke to was Natalie, a French national originally from Congo who had three teenage children and wanted to move the family from France to the UK. Her brother and sister are here and her children want to study in London, but the real reason she wanted to leave France was because the family had been victims of racism. She told me she was attracted by how tolerant and diverse London seemed, where people from every part of the population and from so many different cultures and nationalities feel at home. But increasingly those who are on lower incomes cannot get a home. Nathaniel Mathews told me he feels that nowadays 'Hackney is too posh for poor people – they end up on the periphery', a phrase that brought to mind the *banlieues* of Paris. The *banlieues* are the suburbs. France has all kinds of suburbs but the word for them has become pejorative, meaning slums on the outskirts of the city dominated by immigrants who live in the *cités* – colossal housing projects with very high levels of deprivation.

The term *'banlieue'* was first coined in the 1860s during Baron Haussmann's huge programme of works in Paris, which included the demolition of crowded medieval neighbourhoods and the creation of wide boulevards – incompatible with revolutionary barricades – that Paris is now famous for. His work met with fierce opposition and Napoleon III dismissed him in 1870, but his projects continued and his spatial vision still dominates the city, which is today defined by a wealthy inner core and the outer *banlieues*. This pattern is being replicated in London and in many other UK cities such as Manchester, Liverpool and Leeds. The well-heeled flock to the city centre, living in luxury apartment blocks in gleaming privatized districts being reconfigured entirely for them. Those on low incomes are expelled to peripheral areas and other parts of the country, which are less well-resourced to start off with and come under great pressure for housing, school places and health services, creating a fertile breeding ground for social problems and racism. Jasmine from Focus E15 agreed that poor housing conditions can lead to racism, telling me: 'When it all started and we were told we would be evicted, I was a believer that immigration is the problem – that "they" take all the housing – that's what the media was telling me.' And there's no doubt that's what some people in less affluent neighbourhoods with poorer services do think when they see families from outside the area given homes, fuelled by the rhetoric of some politicians and the well-worn narrative played out in many newspapers. But it's not immigrants and those on low incomes who are responsible for the housing shortage. It's the fact that, when it comes to housing, the market is unable to serve the public good, which in this case is the legal – albeit increasingly limited – duty of local authorities to house people in need near to where they already live.

This public duty is already restricted, with councils having a duty of care only to those in priority need, which covers families with children and people with mental or physical health issues or at risk of domestic abuse. The state has no responsibility to house homeless single people or childless couples, leaving a large 'hidden homeless' population who may be sofa-surfing, sleeping on buses, rough sleeping, in hostels or in illegal accommodation. The numbers are impossible to quantify with any degree of accuracy, not least because some of these people will move in and out of the private rented sector. But while it is difficult to get exact figures, London's Poverty Profile highlights that the number of rough sleepers has increased every year since 2007 and is now double what it was in the mid-2000s, with 7,580 people sleeping rough in London in 2015.[26]

Yet despite the housing crisis, local authority housing waiting lists have been slashed. This is simply councils shifting the goalposts and making it more difficult to qualify as eligible for housing. A survey found that 159 English councils have struck 237,793 people off their lists since 2012 when the Localism Act came into effect, allowing councils to state applicants must have a local connection to the area.[27] For example, despite the housing crisis, Hammersmith and Fulham Council cut its housing waiting list by almost 90 per cent in 2013, from more than 10,000 people to 1,100, after imposing a rule that only those who had lived in the area for more than five years were eligible to apply. With questionable logic, Andrew Johnson, the council's cabinet member for housing, claimed that the real demand was therefore for low-cost home ownership, which he justified by pointing out that since the housing list had been cut the waiting list for intermediate housing was now much bigger.[28]

FROM BRICKS TO BENEFITS: THE RISE OF HOUSING BENEFIT

In 1991, when the then Conservative housing minister Sir George Young was asked in Parliament what the government was going to do about tenants on benefit facing unaffordable rents, he responded that if people could not afford to pay the market rent, 'housing benefit will take the strain'. This went on to become one of the most famous phrases in housing. A leading housing policy official I spoke to said that the necessity for housing benefit to 'take the strain' has been one of the key planks of housing policy since then but that this has now 'been kicked away'. 'That last resort is no longer there,' he said.

A report by Shelter, called 'Bricks or benefits?' makes clear how the rise in the benefit bill is the result of specific decisions made by successive governments to subsidize people on low incomes to live in private rented housing rather than build new social housing. The report states: 'The shift from supply side investment to demand side allowances was in many respects deliberate, and Ministers accepted that the housing benefit bill would "inevitably" rise as the result of housing policies.' But, the report continues, 'it is hard to believe that past governments anticipated the bill would increase to the extent which it has, due in part to rising costs and lack of supply'.[29]

Two other key policies introduced by Margaret Thatcher's government, Right to Buy and Buy to Let, interact with the way housing benefit operates today to push rents up. Buy to Let, brought in alongside housing benefit at the height of the Thatcher era in 1988, came in with the Housing Act of that year, which also removed rent controls and tenant security with the creation of short tenancies. But it only took off in 1996, when Buy to Let mortgages were introduced and a new Housing Act made the short Assured Shorthold Tenancy the main type of tenancy. Today, Buy to Let is booming and in London accounts for a quarter of the mortgage market and nearly half of all newbuild properties, fuelled by demand in every part of the housing market, from professionals to those in housing need.[30] Added to this mix is Right to Buy. This was originally designed to shift wealth to the less well-off, but now often transfers it directly into the pockets of private landlords, as the original beneficiaries of the 'property-owning democracy' sell up, often to professional private landlords. In 2016, a House of Commons Select Committee report found that 40 per cent of former council homes sold through Right to Buy are being rented out far more expensively by private landlords, some of whom own hundreds of properties.[31] When council properties move into the private rented sector the rent increases are extreme, with government figures for 2015 showing the rent for a council two-bed flat was £417 a month[32] compared to £1,500 in the private rented sector.[33]

To top it all off, very often it is the taxpayer who is picking up the tab through the soaring housing benefit bill. Research by the National Housing Federation found that the amount paid by the taxpayer to private landlords doubled from £4.6 billion in 2006 to £9.3 billion in 2016. More than 40 per cent of the entire housing benefit bill goes straight into the pockets of private landlords. The money is not rein-vested in housing, although this booming market is driven by demand from councils who desperately need the properties because they don't have enough social housing. The result is that nearly every local authority operates private sector leasing schemes, leasing back former council properties from private landlords – at huge expense.

Not only are the economics a nonsensical waste of taxpayers' money, conditions are often very poor. As the Select Committee report concluded: 'The potential for selling social housing assets at a discount, only for them to become both more expensive and possibly lower quality housing in the private rented sector, is a significant concern.'[34] A *Dispatches* investigation for Channel 4 called 'Housing Benefit Millionaires' revealed how bad conditions are themselves driven by the dysfunctional market in housing benefit. Landlords are able to charge more than double in housing benefit for a self-contained flat than a room in a shared house. So they put a toilet and the most basic cooking facilities into a room and pick up £1,000 a week for renting out four or five tiny apartments in what is essen-tially a two-bedroom house. In this way 200 landlords and lettings agents across the country have received more than £1 million in housing benefit over the past three years, with B&R Estates, one of the London companies investigated, hoovering up £2 million.[35]

Other cuts to housing benefit are hitting those in social housing and, while the economically dysfunctional impact of cuts to Local Housing Allowance slipped under the radar, the bedroom tax, which affects council and housing association tenants, created a storm of controversy – but little change to the policy. Officially called the 'spare room subsidy', it cuts housing benefit by 14 per cent for one 'spare' room and 25 per cent for two or more. The idea was that the policy would get households to move into smaller properties, but with few available, the main result has been debt and mental and physical health problems with disabled families particularly hard hit, as they often need a spare room for essential home adaptations or equipment to enable them to live independently. Research commissioned by the government itself found households cutting back on essential food and heating. Forty per cent reported being in arrears with their rent, a quarter said they had to borrow money, mostly from friends, and at least 7 per cent cited having to resort to payday loans.[36] When the United Nations Special Rapporteur on housing, Raquel Rolnik, visited the UK in 2013 she reported, to the fury of the UK government, that a number of welfare reforms along with cuts in housing benefits 'appear to compromise the realization of the right to adequate housing and other related human rights'.[37] The final report stated:

> The Special Rapporteur regrets that some policies and practices which have resulted in the progressive realization of the right to adequate housing are being eroded, and that the structural shape of the housing sector has changed to the detriment of the most vulnerable. She expresses her concern that recent measures are contributing to an increased vulnerability of those who, until a few years ago, were protected.

Far from paying any attention to the report, which also recommended that the spare room subsidy be 'suspended immediately',[38] it was roundly condemned by the government as 'a misleading Marxist diatribe'.[39] The *Daily Mail* published a profile of Rolnik headlined: 'Raquel Rolnik: a dabbler in witchcraft who offered an animal sacrifice to Marx'.[40]

Coming at the same time as all these housing benefit cuts are the swingeing 40 per cent cuts imposed on local authorities in 2011 as part of the government's austerity agenda, which aimed to reduce the deficit by enforcing £50 billion in cuts over five years.[41] It's set to get even worse with the Housing and Planning Act. As it became law only in 2016, after a bitterly fought campaign of opposition, its effects will take some time to filter through and it is not yet clear if all the measures will be fully implemented. Even if some of the most extreme are dropped, the trends already described are the future of housing – but in a turbo-charged form that is expected to kill off social housing altogether. Meanwhile, additional cuts in 2016 and 2017 include the end of council tax support for low-income families, cuts to bereavement benefits and the removal of child tax credits for the third and subsequent children. The combined impact will take us back to the Victorian era, before philanthropic pressure and social change created the conditions for large-scale public house building.

5

Generation Rent

TWENTY-FIRST-CENTURY SLUMS

I first met Ian Dick, head of private housing at Newham Council, in 2011 when he took me on an off-the-record walk around East Ham. At that time 'beds in sheds' – illegal structures in back gardens – were a growing problem alongside criminal levels of overcrowding; it was not uncommon to find ten or twenty people living in a room above a fried chicken shop, or in a basement or in sheds.[1] When we met again, five years later, he was happy to talk to me on the record, not because the problems had gone, but because he was proud of the council's private rented sector licensing regime introduced in 2013 – the first in the country – leading to 800 prosecutions and twenty-eight landlords being banned.

This time we met in Forest Gate, which he described as 'the new Hackney'. 'This is an area undergoing the most dramatic change – the council doesn't use the term "gentrification", they use the term "regeneration",' he said as we strolled down a pleasant high street in the sunshine, looking up at Victorian façades renovated by the council, with ground-floor hipster cafés and pubs interspersed with local clothes retailers, halal butchers and phone shops. To show me the reality behind the façades in some of the flats above the shops, he took me around the back, where an entire street was accessed by a badly maintained private alleyway, with a huge pile of mattresses dumped at one end. The mattresses were outside a property where twenty people had been living the previous week, under a structure in the yard outside. 'The landlord is under caution, he's not arrested,

Nico and Jakub are Property Guardians in Croydon. They had to paint and furnish the property themselves; in return they pay 60 per cent of market value in rent. They can be evicted with a notice period of only one month and the landlord has access to the property at any time.

he's been housing people desperate for accommodation – people were paying £400 a month for this,' Ian explained. Further down the back alley, the entrances to a large number of flats were up dangerous-looking fire escape stairs, particularly hazardous for children. In one of the properties a scooter stood at the foot of a rickety open stairway with just a central rail for support.

But, for me, the most upsetting place we saw was at the back of a large Victorian house with a smell of leaking sewage, the once white walls now filthy and soot stained. 'This must be illegal. That's the thing about English housing – there's little that's illegal but there'll be breaches here,' he explained, telling me that English property law does not target property standards but that interventions can be made around public health. In this case the breaches would be drainage and conditions detrimental to health. 'This is the sort of private rented sector that still exists in 2016, even after all we've done,' he said, noting details down in his notebook for his officers to visit. The interior to one of the flats was visible through a grim-looking security gate at the back door. Through the bars I could see a toddler and his mother. This was no place for a child – or anyone – to live but it was also obvious that once they were evicted their fortunes might not necessarily improve because there would be nowhere to go, and even if they qualified for housing they would most likely enter the world of substandard temporary accommodation in places like Boundary House.

Walking back down the high street we paused to look at some of the 'to let' signs in the newsagents' windows. One in particular stood out, offering a room share for four people for £160 a month, effectively a bed space in what may or may not be legal accommodation. Renting bed spaces, I had already heard from a number of sources, is becoming a more common way of renting, with bunk beds visible in the front rooms of nearby terraces. While we sat having a coffee, Ian explained this was partly down to the phenomenon of 'rent to rent'. 'There's a whole submarket in rent to rent. An estate agent will rent a house to an individual who will then let it out to others, who might also sublet. It's all done with no documentation, they don't ask for references, and when we go round we might find fifteen people there.'

There's different levels of this going on – everybody has to share because nobody can afford to rent,' he said, adding that sometimes criminal gangs are involved, who might rent twenty properties, and then re-rent them at a 20 per cent higher price. Incredulous, I said that surely reputable estate agents wouldn't be involved, to which he replied that the council had prosecuted twenty-five agents, and pointed to a clue as to how to find them, through the ads in local papers: 'It's in the local paper ads, where you see agents offer "guaranteed rent" – there are no controls on lettings agents.'

Since Newham introduced its licensing scheme, the council has put a maximum limit on the number of people allowed per room and has stipulated that agents must display what that limit is, although some don't. 'Lots of them were non-compliant at the beginning but when we looked at them they started to comply, and then we relaxed and they went back to what they were doing before,' Ian said. It doesn't surprise him: 'Why wouldn't they? The housing market is broken and the conditions are ripe for exploitation. We've got the worst of both worlds – a market which is controlled but not regulated.' Given what's going on, I asked him whether the licensing scheme had made any difference. 'It could have got a lot worse – we've held the line. Most people we've prosecuted are criminal landlords, although the government prefer the term "rogue",' he replied.

With the help of the licensing scheme, the burgeoning problem of beds in sheds, which was one of Ian's biggest concerns when we first met in 2011, is less severe and he is at least aware of some of the worst housing conditions. But the 'beds in sheds' have not gone away, they've just migrated. A report on the subject in 2015 by the London Borough of Redbridge states:

> The mass emergence of unauthorised dwellings located within rear gardens (Beds in Sheds), once thought to be concentrated in inner London Boroughs has now seen a significant migration to outer London and the suburbs. Many now fear that a new hidden community has emerged, on a scale much greater than initially suspected. The outbuildings which families can now be found

occupying in our borough may be paralleled to the type of Victorian era back to back dwellings constructed as a result of mass urbanisation, and which were ultimately subject to wholesale demolition during the mass slum clearances of major cities in the 1930s and post war periods.[2]

The report detailed how the council carried out 326 inspections of suspected occupied outbuildings in Redbridge, and found that 181 people – of which thirty-five were children or infants – were living in them, although it added that a significantly higher number showed evidence of suspected occupancy. 'It is believed that many rogue landlords removed occupants either by relocation or illegal eviction prior to inspection,' the report stated. It concluded that on the basis of information gathered by the Metropolitan Police, borough-wide there might be 1,000–2,000 'bed in shed' structures. Particularly concerning to the authors of the report were the associated offences, such as tax fraud, exploitation, profiteering from illegal immigrants and human trafficking, which are becoming increasingly identified with rogue landlords. According to estimates, there are up to 13,000 human trafficking victims in the UK,[3] and typical traffickers' methods of control, such as removing their documentation and passports and periodically relocating them from one place to another to isolate them, apply here. The report states:

> With this level of control, victims become helpless and have almost no chance of escaping. These circumstances are regularly reflected in officer findings when attending occupied outbuildings. It is often found that occupants are not in possession of identification such as passport or travel documents. They will usually state that these documents are in the possession of someone else . . . the occupants will often communicate and respond to questions with clearly coached answers.

This is happening all over London. In Southwark, Councillor Mark Williams told me that the council found a two-bedroom flat on the Aylesbury Estate with twenty occupants, who were being bussed down to Bromley every day to work in a sweatshop. 'We think broadly a third of landlords are well meaning and do a good job, a third are well meaning and do a bad job and a third are rogue landlords, and at the fringes of that you have slum landlords and criminal human trafficking,' he said. Although it is notoriously difficult to get accurate figures, a 2013 report by the Migrants' Rights Network concluded that Ealing may have as many as 60,000 occupants in illegal structures, and Slough, which deployed planes to fly over the town using thermal imaging equipment to try to spot them, may have as many as 6,000 beds in sheds. The report noted that there is anecdotal evidence both of traffickers accommodating their victims in illegal structures and of trafficked victims who manage to escape resorting to this sort of accommodation.[4] Estate agents are also linked to the problem: a BBC investigation found estate agents renting out beds in sheds in Willesden Green in Brent and Wembley in Harrow.[5]

Newham's licensing scheme has been widely praised, with many councils wanting to emulate it. But in 2015, to the delight of the landlord lobby, the government made it clear it did not want to extend its use, with then housing minister Brandon Lewis calling licensing a 'tenants tax'.[6] Even though the Department for Communities and Local Government had given Newham £1 million to support the licensing scheme, little-known changes to the law, introduced through secondary legislation, have seen 'selective licensing' extended but also made it much harder, if not impossible, for councils to introduce licensing in the first place, with the new law ensuring that councils have to seek permission from the secretary of state for any licensing scheme which would cover more than 20 per cent of their geographical area, or affect more than 20 per cent of privately rented homes. As a result, housing charity Shelter said that 'although not explicitly ruling out borough-wide selective licensing, this new measure is designed to put a stop to this practice'.[7] In Redbridge, for example, the secretary of state refused the council's application for borough-wide licensing and as a result council leader Jas Athwal said it would be 'impossible for us to readily identify who is responsible for a property and deal proactively with poor standards of rented accommodation'.[8] So, although an effective means has been found of clamping down on terrible housing conditions, the government does not support it.

MIDDLE-CLASS POVERTY

Extreme overcrowding through rent to rent and beds in sheds are illegal. But poor conditions in the 'mainstream' private rented sector are also commonplace. Jan is a university graduate with a good job who lives in what she describes as 'middle-class poverty' despite earning close to £40,000 a year. She explained her family's situation to me, hit by a double whammy of frequent evictions and not enough money to make ends meet, even though both she and her partner work full time. Her despairing post on social media opens this book because it reflects a situation which is now all too frequent across London. The family's most recent move – they last moved three years ago when their old landlord increased the rent by £450 a month – is because this landlord has sold the two flats in the house they lived in to a developer who plans to turn it into one luxury house. Conditions where they were living were far from ideal, with heating that didn't work properly and Jan and her partner sleeping in the front room so that their two children, a ten-year-old boy and seven-year-old girl, could have their own rooms. But that isn't possible in the tiny two-bedroom flat they're in now, so she is thinking of putting a mattress in the alcove in the hallway for her daughter. 'I'm going to put a curtain up and have her in that, but when I think about that, it's Dickensian,' she said. Revealing how she has adjusted her expectations to far below what she would have once considered acceptable, she added, 'We're in a flat which is substandard accommodation but what we love about it is that the heating works.' The other advantage is that the overcrowded, moth-infested flat is cheaper, meaning that for the first time in years she will be able to pay off her overdraft, but it is in the wrong catchment area for the secondary school her son has applied to, which is causing him great anxiety. The estate agent, who she says looks out for them, has found her a larger flat in West Norwood where they used live, but that would, as before, eat up two-thirds of her salary. 'We can stay here and clear our overdraft or go back to West Norwood, have a kitchen diner and live totally beyond our means. It's these ridiculous choices,' she explained. The other option would be moving to Croydon or Mitcham, but prices aren't much cheaper there. 'We might be able to get a semi with a garden but the kids would not be in the catchment area for their schools, there's a massive commute and you lose all your networks.'

Jan is paid far above the average salary and her partner, who is a teaching assistant, also has a full-time job. But after the cost of child-care is deducted, they have nothing left to spare – 'it's second-hand clothes and no holidays. It's middle-class poverty – they call it "the squeezed middle" but it's poverty. It impacts on a whole range of things you can't begin to anticipate,' she said. To cap it all, on the day we met she'd had a terrible journey into work with cancelled trains and her Oyster card charging her an extra £20 by mistake, which she simply didn't have. 'I just stood on the platform crying. It's beyond my capacity to cope with it. I just can't cope with any of it,' she told me as we sat in her large office in Clerkenwell. 'Look at where I work – I earn all of this money yet our situation is pitiful.'

For the last generation Britain's economy and culture have been predicated on the ideal of home ownership, fuelled by the Conservative vision of a property-owning democracy. But despite the mythology, Britain exceeded the European average of 70 per cent home ownership only in the early noughties. It has now fallen to 64 per cent, the lowest level in thirty years; the last time home ownership was this low was in 1986, when Right to Buy and the deregulation of the mortgage market were sending home ownership upwards. As home ownership falls and social housing is eradicated, expensive private renting is becoming the only option: in 2017 private renting overtook mortgaged home ownership in London.[9] 'This is a middle-class issue now, that people want to talk about,' Betsy Dilner, director of Generation Rent, the campaign group for better private renting, told me, although she added: 'People think we represent this middle-class professional group, but if you can find a way of making the private rented sector work for the most vulnerable people in society then it will work for everyone.' Today, 11 million people in

Britain rent privately in an overlapping series of submarkets ranging from the poor conditions and slum housing at the bottom end to student accommodation, micro 'pocket living' flats, apartments for professionals and luxury housing at the top.[10]

About a third of Britain's private renters are on housing benefit, a third according to Dilner would like to buy their own home and a third would be quite happy renting if the rental market worked properly, as it does in many other European countries like Germany, where rents are a modest 23 per cent of earnings compared to more than half in London. She thinks the sector is broken at every level and believes change must focus on the four key areas of affordability, management, security and decent conditions. To achieve this Generation Rent would like to see rent controls, a national register of landlords and fully licensed lettings agents – all of which Dilner admits is highly unlikely in the current ideological climate. 'There are more requirements to run a cattery than to rent out a home. There should be regulations to look after pets but I'd like the same rights to be afforded to the place we call home every day,' she said.

Like 2.3 million other Londoners, Green Party London Assembly member Sian Berry is a private renter, who has shelled out more than half her pay in rent and lived in six different houses since she moved to London twenty years ago. In 2016, she published a 'Big Renters Survey' of more than 1,000 renters who described their experiences, highlighting rocketing rents compared to wages, poor conditions and the way lettings agents and landlords treat them.[11] Rising rents were the most common problem experienced in the previous three years, and seven in ten renters suffered from repairs and maintenance not being done. Damp, mould, broken boilers and dangerous electrics feature prominently in the responses, with many reports of landlords who evict tenants rather than carry out repairs. One said: 'After thousands of pounds' worth of electrical items all broke down at once, an electrician assessed our flat. He found that the wiring was the worst he'd ever seen and was, in his words a "death trap". We were living there with a new-born baby. Our landlord chose to evict us, making us homeless, rather than carry out repairs.' Another one reported that they had to wear rubber gloves in the shower to avoid electric shocks and a third described how: 'Once a ceiling of an old house fell on me and all my stuff. I let my landlady send workers into the house to fix it for two months, during which time we still had to pay some rent. Immediately afterwards she put the rent up to a level we could not afford and we had to move out.' The problem of rising rents elicited this typical response: 'Most recent move was due to landlord putting the rent up by 35 per cent. He had put it up by smaller amounts every year and it was already hard to afford.' There is even unhappiness at the very highest echelons of the market: the wife of Bank of England governor Mark Carney sparked opprobrium when she tweeted that she couldn't find anywhere affordable to live in London, despite his £5,000 a week housing allowance.

The phenomenal growth of Airbnb is another factor putting pressure on rents as it removes properties from the rental market while keeping prices high. Airbnb is becoming the focus of housing activists across Europe and in the US, particularly in cities which attract large numbers of tourists, such as New York, Barcelona, Berlin – and London. In Barcelona and Berlin the city government has banned renting out whole properties through Airbnb, and at the time of writing the company was embroiled in a battle in New York over the same issue. But while regulation is being introduced, it is a notoriously hard business to regulate and raises contentious issues in a city such as Barcelona where it has become an important source of income for people on modest salaries. The success of the model fits perfectly into Thomas Piketty's thesis that income from rent now far exceeds economic growth, let alone wages. As such, it is likely to remain a key feature of the contemporary property market.

The bedroom tax presents a mirror image of Airbnb. In a society where the ideal of public housing has collapsed, a financial penalty is imposed on people in social housing with a spare room, while those who are lucky enough to own a house with one find themselves with an additional source of revenue. Another feature of the new economy in private renting is property guardianship, where developers offer lower rents to people prepared to live in properties due to be redeveloped. Often these are in edgy locations such as Goldfinger's Balfron Tower in East London, and the community of artists who move in briefly also brings a cachet which adds to the appealing nature of an area in the throes of change. In the past artists squatted in abandoned buildings in places such as Hoxton and Shoreditch in East London and Brixton in South London in a process that has long been credited with maintaining diversity in cities while also unwittingly kick-starting a slower process of gentrification in those areas. But in 2013 legislation was passed which made squatting in residential buildings illegal, and property guardianship can be seen as an attempt to co-opt the perceived desirable elements of squatting by artists in a blatant bid to accelerate gentrification. At the same time, it is a highly lucrative, unregulated business, and guardians, who have no property rights, often have to put up with poor conditions and can be evicted at short notice.

The major concern for the government and employers in London is that people will simply not put up with the extortionate rents and leave, hollowing out the city and threatening its labour market and culture. 'We see this with employers saying they're having a really hard time retaining professional level jobs, let alone cleaners. London is losing teachers – they're commuting from Luton and they're giving up – it's having a massive knock-on effect,' Dilner said. The vacancy rate for nurses at London's hospitals is 14–18 per cent according to a report from health think tank the King's Fund, and the number of entrants to teacher training has fallen 16 per cent since 2010 according to Ofsted.[12] But it's not just carers, nurses, teachers, doctors, artists and university lecturers who can't afford London. Fifty Thousand Homes is a business-led campaign group which includes the Royal Bank of Scotland, the CBI and scores of London's businesses, formed to push the housing crisis up the political agenda. Their research shows that on current trends customer services and sales staff at almost every level will be pushed out, with 73 per cent of businesses believing London's housing costs are a significant risk to the capital's economic growth and 70 per cent of Londoners aged twenty-five to thirty-nine reporting that the cost of their rent or mortgage makes it difficult to work in London.[13]

Vicky Spratt is a 28-year old journalist who worked as a producer of political programmes at the BBC but left because she felt the issues affecting her generation, like the housing crisis, were not being covered properly. 'A lot of issues were dismissed by the older genera-tion – it didn't affect them. They all owned their own homes,' she told me. She joined the digital lifestyle magazine *The Debrief*, aimed at twenty-something women, and began a campaign against lettings agents' fees which was so successful it gathered more than 250,000 signatures. As a result, Chancellor Philip Hammond banned lettings agents' fees in his 2016 Autumn Statement, which is the biggest vic-tory for private renters to date. Spratt, who describes herself as a reluctant campaigner, had never done anything like this before, but she was fed up. She currently pays £1,430 per month, not including bills, for a one-bedroom flat which she can afford because she shares with her boyfriend, but she also told me how she used to live in a room 'which was literally the size of a bed'. 'I noticed after six to eight weeks my mental health deteriorated, the walls were very thin because it had originally been part of one room which the landlord split into two. If I wasn't in a relationship I would be looking at going back to that,' she said.

Like Jan, Spratt earns enough to get a mortgage but, because rents are so high, not enough to save for the 20–30 per cent deposit required. 'The common thread for people my age is that we don't own our own homes and potentially we never will. The housing cri-sis is older than me and it shocks me that nobody did anything about this and I want it on the news agenda,' she said. 'This is structural neglect. The buy to let boom and the unregulated market has a lot to answer for – it's not like this in other countries, there are checks in place and a different way of looking at property.' She believes a key reason for this political failure is that 'people who don't experience this issue are in charge', pointing out that a third of MPs are buy to let landlords. An Oxford graduate who has worked in Westminster, she also suspects that a factor behind the success of her campaign is because 'I look and sound like them'.

People facing sky-high rents are being forced out of many US cit-ies, including New York, San Francisco, Seattle and Portland, where Generation Rent's Dilner is from and where similar battles are played out, as they are in other British cities such as Manchester and Bristol.

'This is the neoliberal free market ideology which has been alive and well in the US for a long time and it is certainly taking over here,' Dilner said. She fears that the outcome will be that the city will become soulless, 'a place where you can't raise families, be young, start up new businesses – all those things that make the city we love – housing costs will suck the soul out of that'.

One of the consequences of the exodus from London is that the same pattern of property speculation and displacement is spreading to other cities such as Bristol, Hastings and Margate. And while population shifts to other towns might seem to some like a good way of rebalancing the economy, the problem is that the majority of the jobs remain in London; nearly every FTSE 100 company is headquartered in the capital. With a weak private sector in the regions and existing public sector jobs shrinking rapidly as a result of cuts to public services, it is not possible to contemplate real solutions to the housing crisis without profound structural economic change. And while some will leave the city, others like Jan will put up with conditions which should be unacceptable, in order to keep their jobs and family ties. This means generation rent must pay through the nose to live in an increasingly hollowed out, sterile city which provides a playground for the rich in the centre, hipster gentrifying areas in the hinterlands and poor housing for cheap labour in our *banlieues*, in parts of Barking and Dagenham or Edmonton where the 'working poor' live.[14]

HOUSING AND MENTAL HEALTH

It is a truism that moving house is the third most stressful life event. It's rarely an easy experience even when the move is voluntary and wanted. But it's incomparably worse when it involves being wrenched away from the support networks, daily routines and the sense of identity that comes with being able to call a place a home. Even the threat of having to move – 'housing insecurity' as it's known – is a significant contributor to mental health problems.

Aysen Denis, a tenant on the Aylesbury, broke down in tears as she described to me how the threat of losing their homes was affecting the community. 'It's affecting people's mental health. It's affecting me emotionally – I don't want to lose my home and my community. When I think, if it happens . . . emotionally I can't understand it, this is my home,' she said. Although she had lived there for twenty-three years she still felt she needed to justify why she was so upset, explaining: 'My father was in the army, we never stayed in the same place for more than two or three years – this is an issue for me. I do need stability and they're taking it away from me.'

Jane Rendell is a Professor of Architecture and Art at the Bartlett School of Architecture. She met Aysen when she was asked to be an expert witness at the public inquiry on the future of the Aylesbury. She also lives nearby, on the neighbouring Wyndham Estate, which is not currently under threat of demolition though it falls within the council's 'development zone'. Speaking to a packed room of activists, academics and local residents at a conference in Southwark in 2016, Rendell described the 'anger and emotional state' in communities across London. 'When we talk about housing and home it links to an emotional state. People are suffering, there's major depression. If we follow some of these plans we'll see a wave of depression moving across London – it's not a weather depression but a psychic depression,' she said in a powerful speech. When I met her soon after, she admitted she didn't know how she would cope if her own home came under threat. 'I just don't know what I'd do. Sell – I don't want to sell. It feels like selling out and I don't want to move to Folkestone and commute, which is what I'd have to do. But I don't think I could handle the stress the Aylesbury residents are going through.'[15]

Psychiatrists and mental health professionals have long understood that the stability of housing is of fundamental importance – according to psychiatrist Dr Ciaran Abbey, it is 'the most important factor'. Abbey and Dr T.B.S. Balamurali are the authors of 'Housing the Mind', a recent study highlighting the importance of security of tenure to general security and wellbeing. The report cites studies which show that prolonged periods in temporary accommodation adversely affect mental health, and evidence that spending more than 30 per cent of income on housing is associated with worse mental health. 'When a disproportionate amount of income is spent on housing, this leaves people less able to purchase other necessities such as adequate food, increasing the family's vulnerability to disease but also the anxiety and sense of helplessness that results when unable to make ends meet.'[16]

A report by social action centre Cambridge House and Leicester University investigated the mental health of clients whose cases have been taken on by the Housing Law Centre at Cambridge House. It highlighted how housing insecurity can both bring about mental health problems and exacerbate existing ones. A man with a history of anxiety, depression and psychosis fell into rent arrears after his business got into difficulties. Still considered fit for work, he had his housing benefit stopped. 'I was physically fit and they didn't diagnose my mental state – they cancelled my ESA and then I got further depressed and wouldn't come out of my house for a couple of weeks,' he explained. The judge in his case queried why benefits are stopped when people are obviously in need and ruled that the defendant pay back his arrears on a weekly basis, which he agreed to do by borrowing from friends. The next case was that of a care worker on a zero hours contract who had a grown-up son living with her who suffered from anxiety and depression. She got into arrears because her zero hours contract meant her hours were not consistent and, although she was eligible for housing benefit, there was a query on her case. Asked if the day in court meant she would be more likely to pay the rent, she said: 'I was never in dispute of it; I just simply don't have enough money. I go to bed every night with a sandwich and a cup of tea [still crying], I can't even have a proper meal . . . I understand it's got to be done, but urgh . . . it just feels like a punishment for the poor. If I was in Dickensian times I would be in a debtors' prison,' she said through tears.[17]

Issues of helplessness and loss of control are at the heart of these findings, as at the core of Abbey and Balamurali's work. This loss of control results in what the psychiatrists describe as 'learned helplessness', the inability to influence one's environment or experiences, and can lead to physical and mental health problems, such as anxiety and depression – an accurate description of the case studies and Jan,

Terry and Brenda's experiences. Housing and home are not just about bricks and mortar, but about identity, emotional security and a sense of place in the world. This is what academics call 'ontological security', a sense of order and continuity in relation to experiences. When individuals lose their homes, they can lose not just their physical shelter but their entire world. Nothing is more devastating to people than losing their identity and that is very closely tied up with home.

6

The 'Right to the City'

The combination of global capital, government policies designed to kill off social housing and failures in housing benefit are reconfiguring the city. The politics of space is replacing the traditional politics of class. The old hierarchy of upper, middle and working class, which ranked groups in society as workers and bosses, no longer holds up in the face of a property-based economy where the income from rent far exceeds economic growth and wages. There is more wealth coming into London than ever before, but these riches are not shared, with unaffordable property prices and rents making life worse for the majority. But as this spatial injustice sweeps the city, there is growing support for an alternative approach, based on the idea of the 'Right to the City', which is able to point towards a way out of the housing crisis, bring down prices and strengthen communities. A profoundly inclusive vision, its great strength is that it provides a framework for alternatives to the extreme emphasis on market conditions. It is based on widespread democratic participation and the reinvigoration of a culture of local politics that includes rather than excludes local people and communities.*

In the US, Right to the City is also the name of an influential campaign movement which emerged in 2007 as a response to

* First coined by the French sociologist Henri Lefebvre, in his 1968 book of the same name, *Le Droit à la ville*, which translates as 'The Right to the City', which was a very important influence on the *soixante-huitards* of the 1968 student protest movement. It built on Lefebvre's earlier work on the production of space and place, which investigated how the places of the city are contested and produced by conflicting socioeconomic and cultural forces.

Sylvia's Corner in Stratford was founded by young mums facing eviction from Newham. Alongside other housing groups they are finding a voice on the national stage.

gentrification, aiming to halt the displacement from communities of people on lower incomes. Now a global movement, the concept was included for the first time in the UN's New Urban Agenda, agreed in Quito, Ecuador, in 2016, which enshrined the 'right to the city' vision in the legislation, political declarations and charters of national and local governments. As such it represented a very significant victory for civil society groups battling against gentrification, repossessions, the privatization of public space and the criminalization of homelessness.* Today, the right to the city is an intellectual idea, campaign slogan, political ideal and legislative mechanism which can help to answer the question posed by this book: who is the city for? Is it for teachers, doctors, taxi drivers and families or is it just for wealthy finance professionals and young people prepared to live in micro flats or substandard accommodation?

There are two approaches to solving the housing crisis, which can be summarized as incremental change or a paradigm shift. The backdrop to both routes is the possibility that the crisis will continue to get worse, whether or not there is a significant downturn in the housing market. At the time of writing in 2017, average house prices were 5.8 per cent lower than at their peak in 2014[1] and there were indications that the prime market in luxury apartments was cooling. Foxtons, an estate agent that focuses exclusively on London, predicted that annual profits would almost halve and forecast that conditions would remain 'challenging'. A senior property industry commentator told me: 'It's a phoney market because interest rates are so low. There is a great big crash on its way but we can't say when it will happen. Asking prices are way too high, nothing is selling.' But although a housing market crash would reduce prices, they are now so high that it would make little difference to most Londoners. Indeed, the economic instability and possible increase in interest rates would likely tighten the mortgage market. Meanwhile, the speculative model underpinning the

---

* These groups came together during the Habitat III process under an advocacy platform called the 'Global Platform for the Right to the City', championed by Brazil and Ecuador, which have already enshrined the right to the city in law at national level. Though not perfect, the final wording was still considered a significant victory.

British housebuilding industry means that a drop in land and property prices would cause housebuilders to stop building, which doesn't solve the crisis either. There are signs this is happening, with developers quick to complete schemes they have already begun but radically slowing the number of 'starts'. Fewer homes will in turn add more pressure on a housing market already unable to cope and will drive further increases in rents.

Opting to pursue the incremental change route is close to aspects of the policies pursued by London's Labour mayors, Ken Livingstone and since 2016 Sadiq Khan. As for Boris Johnson, while Gordon Brown was in power, he too followed this route before altering course dramatically when the Conservative-led coalition was elected and his old rival Livingstone was out of the picture. When Boris was fighting against Ken to win his second term, he got headlines for condemning the 'Kosovo-style social cleansing' which saw people on housing benefit being pushed out of London.[2] But as chapter 4 described, under his watch this trend – which he stopped referring to in his second term – became far more entrenched, and not long after he was elected he was making lavish declarations of approval for the oligarchs' cranes which he described as 'marvellous'.[3]

The main thrust of Livingstone's approach, which Sadiq Khan is indicating he would like to emulate, was to raise the numbers of affordable housing that developers have to provide. This was a real political priority for Livingstone, who did manage to get developers to build between 35 and 50 per cent affordable housing. Even then, there was no net gain in affordable housing in London, although overall housing numbers did go up. Sadiq Khan is operating in a far less favourable political climate, under a Conservative government which wants to all but eradicate social housing 'apart from a tiny percentage of social rent for older people and people with disabilities', according to a seasoned observer.[4] Khan stood on a mayoral platform of providing genuinely affordable housing. But his powers are very limited because they mainly impact on newly built housing and that accounts for only a tiny 0.7 per cent of existing housing in London. New homes account for a slightly higher figure of 14.5 per cent of all homes sold and Khan has indicated he plans to get developers to build a similar percentage of affordable housing in new developments as under Livingstone. But not all of these will really be affordable to Londoners on lower incomes. Nor is it easy to understand what is on offer with the affordable housing which does get built divided into an impossibly confusing range of different 'products'. These include shared ownership and part-rent part-buy, social rent and his much trailed plans to introduce a new London Living Rent based on a third of average local incomes, which is a rent to buy product with tenants encouraged to save for homes that will revert to shared ownership after ten years.

Persuading developers to build even this amount of affordable housing will not be easy. The way Khan plans to do this is to make it clear to developers that if they agree, their financial viability assessments won't be scrutinized, but if they raise objections, their schemes are likely to flounder because the other power the mayor has is that he can 'call in' schemes and refuse planning permission for developments that are not in tune with what he wants. This would also send an important symbolic message about the kind of city his administration wishes to preside over, aiming to avoid creating places like Elephant Park which have barely any affordable housing at all. While this is welcome, given the scale of the crisis it feels more like rearranging the deck chairs on the *Titanic* than providing real alternatives, a reality perhaps reflected by the comments from the mayor's housing adviser, James Murray, that 'this is a marathon, not a sprint'.[5]

Only a paradigm shift in British housing policy will be able to address the housing crisis and the failure to provide homes Londoners can afford, which is such an important part of Right to the City's agenda. The planning system is not equipped to deal with the severity of the situation, with Section 106 failing to build anything like the number of affordable homes needed since it was introduced more than twenty-five years ago. The inclusion of the right to the city as part of the UN's New Urban Agenda is important to the UK as the housing crisis is now so serious that new legislative solutions and levers are needed. We must re-examine the operation of property and land markets and their interaction with taxation and the planning system and the marketization of the benefits system. Devolution of powers at local authority and city and regional level should also have a far greater role to play than they do at present.

Given the extent of the challenge, and the direction of travel of current policy towards yet further financialization, enabling this shift in political culture cannot be separated from the vital importance of democratic renewal. The undermining of democracy, where communities are routinely ignored and excluded from key decisions, is also part of the housing crisis. Whole swathes of the city are being removed from the debate. It is only by giving these communities a voice that their right to the city can be realized.

DEMOCRATIC RENEWAL

> No sooner do you set foot on American soil, than you find yourself in a sort of tumult . . . here the people of a district are assembled . . . there they are busy choosing a representative; further on the delegates of a district are hurrying to town to consult about some local improvements . . . one group of citizens assembles for the sole object of announcing they disapprove of the government's course, while others unite to claim that the men in office are the fathers of their country.
>
> Alexis de Tocqueville, *Democracy in America*

The closest I've come to Tocqueville's description of citizens' assemblies and democracy in nineteenth-century America was when I visited Barcelona and met activists involved with the PAH, which translates as the Platform for People Affected by Mortgages. Formed in Barcelona in the aftermath of the financial crisis, the PAH is a civil society movement of volunteers with 200 branches across Spain which meet in weekly assemblies. The strength of the PAH is to a large degree the result of the severity of the housing crisis that led to hundreds of thousands of people being made homeless when their homes were repossessed. It's also the result of a strategy that has combined a campaign of civil disobedience with the pursuit of legislative and political change.

In the UK, despite the turbulence of recent political events, civil society remains strong, as reflected by the 12.7 million people who regularly undertake voluntary work, sit on parish councils or help out on the boards of charitable organizations. And as in Spain, the strength of civil society is also reflected in the mushrooming of many thousands of protest groups fighting to protect their communities from decisions they feel have been made without their consent, with campaign groups often supported by a wide range of professionals such as architects creating alternative community plans or solicitors and barristers giving their expertise *pro bono*. This wave of protest and participation includes battles against hospital closures and in support of junior doctors, the anti-fracking movement, opposition to airport expansion and the range of issues related to the housing crisis. Many of these are achieving some success, from the legal battles around the proposed demolition of estates to successful rent strikes on university campuses that have forced universities to negotiate and agree lower rents for students. At the same time groups like the Radical Housing Network, 35 per cent, Just Space and Focus E15 are finding a voice on the national stage.

As the success of the PAH activists in Spain has shown, when the situation becomes severe, then the chances of change also increase. It is perhaps no coincidence that the most successful housing movement in Europe is in a country which lived under General Franco's dictatorship until 1976: the struggle for democratic rights is still alive in people's memories, in a way that it no longer is in the UK. The scale of the financial crisis in Spain, where 350,000 homes were repossessed, also served to bring together the housing movement. It is comparatively disparate in London, focused on local struggles and lacking the resources to link up despite the emergence of successful umbrella groups. Even so, there are also many parallels, especially as the focus of the PAH is now shifting away from repossessions and towards the crisis in renting. Sitting in a café in the centre of Barcelona, I spent an afternoon talking to Santi, a PAH activist, who told me that renting was at a critical point. 'Every week we have an assembly and the main reason people come now is because they are being evicted because they can't pay the rent. In Barcelona 95 per cent of evictions are because of rents,' he explained.

Despite the crisis, he also described how the combination of civil disobedience and the pressure for legislative change, backed by a powerful communications and social media presence, has led to real results. The group publicize and stop evictions at the rate of fifty a week and occupy banks on a weekly basis, with the consequence that banks now negotiate with them. 'We retake empty homes from banks and we put families in them. We say, "if you come to the PAH we will give you a home" and we have housed 2,500 people,' he told me, referring to the PAH's 'Obra Social Campaign', which frees up empty houses held by financial institutions and places families in them who have been repossessed or evicted. The PAH's 'Stop Evictions Campaign' describes their methods, which include talks and negotiations with banks, outreach to public administration offices to mediate and provide social housing in the event of an eviction and campaigns through social networks and mass media. It is only if none of the above works that a public callout to physically resist evictions goes out and is widely publicized.[6] In 2015, the People's Legislative Initiative against evictions and the cutting off of utilities, promoted by the PAH, was passed unanimously by the Catalonian government and was in place for a year. However, the decision at national level was adjourned, which means the initiative is no longer in force, but it shows what can be done. With the ongoing activities of Goldman Sachs and private equity firms such as Blackstone at the forefront of high-profile evictions in Madrid, now brought to national attention by the PAH, this is a very live issue in Spain and their attempts to change the system are at the top of the Spanish political agenda.

In 2014, Ada Colau, a leading PAH activist, was elected mayor of Barcelona and other PAH members became members of the city government. They immediately left the PAH so as not to compromise its independence and since then the relationship between activists and government has reflected the tensions progressive governments are often faced with in power. 'Six months after Ada came to power we wrote a letter to her saying we were not happy and that created a situation. We are all learning,' Santi said. 'From the beginning she said, "I need you on the streets," but when we do it she doesn't feel that comfortable. But it's the best [outcome] that could happen for us,' he continued. Colau's own definition of the democratic city is that it 'is in permanent conflict and permanent construction. The point is to be really open; to keep innovating, listening to citizens,' she wrote after the UN's inclusion of the 'Right to the City' concept,[7] echoing the arguments of French sociologist Henri Lefebvre, who believed that city space is, and should be, contested. It is likely that in London too, as the crisis in renting continues to get worse, it will also become the main focus for change.

Throughout the UK, there is a renewed enthusiasm for local and national politics, partly in response to greater political and economic uncertainty and partly in response to the feeling that the views of local communities are not listened to. When I shared a platform with Chris Walker, the influential director of Policy Exchange, he said, to the fury of much of the audience: 'In the past, we've had a system where local people can say no to local development. That now is beginning to change.' This reveals just how great the barriers to democratic participation are. There are many routes democratic renewal could take in the UK, which could involve a variety of strategies with regard to 'right to the city' issues, from the wave of protest groups against evictions to the civil disobedience of occupations and rent strikes. But democratic renewal cannot be just about protest, it must also involve a rethinking of our institutions, particularly with regard to the media, where the failure of local accountability in the consultation process accompanying development projects described earlier in this book goes hand in hand with a media in which standards of journalistic scrutiny have collapsed.

Thirty years ago newspapers had housing and planning correspondents and local papers, which covered mainly council matters and crime, helped expose scandals of national significance, such as the fall of former Newcastle council leader T. Dan Smith, on charges of corruption linked to payments received by his PR company. Today, the majority of local papers are owned by a small number of corporations such as Newsquest, which is a subsidiary of the

American group Gannett Co. Inc. – owner of ninety newspapers and twenty-three TV stations in the US – which owns more than 200 local papers in the UK. The main impact of corporate ownership has been to slash staff costs and resources, while at the same time the role PR and lobbying plays in every journalist's life, whether in the local or national media, has grown exponentially.[8] This is partly because of the huge resources ploughed into PR and partly because the cuts mean journalists no longer have the time to research stories properly. According to the Public Relations Consultants Association, the PR and Communications industries have 83,000 employees compared to 45,000 employed journalists, and figures from the Labour Force Survey 2015 revealed a 6,000 drop in journalist numbers compared to an 18,000 rise in PRs over the previous two years.[9] The resulting lack of scrutiny is abundantly clear to see, not least when it comes to the media's stance on contentious development decisions. For example, in Aberdeenshire, the *Press and Journal* and its sister paper, the *Evening Express*, took an aggressively pro-Trump stance in covering the plans for his controversial golf course. The seven councillors who had refused the golf course application were pictured on the front page under the headline 'You traitors' and the paper's editorial, 'Betrayed by the stupidity of the seven', described the councillors as 'misfits' and 'small-minded numpties', with the partisan coverage making no attempt to present their arguments fairly.[10] As to London's own newspaper, the *Evening Standard*, its 'Homes and Property' section is little more than 'advertorial' alongside pages and pages of property listings and the paper has long been a cheerleader for the turbo-charged development of the city.

The creep of actual advertorial into even well-respected news outlets equally raises questions about the need to hold powerful interests to account. For example, the *Guardian*'s website includes a 'paid content' section which features a number of articles by Lendlease, with the *Guardian*'s masthead at the top and laid out in the *Guardian*'s design. One of the pieces, headlined 'Smart urban regeneration projects put people and partnerships first', is by Dan Labbad, chief executive officer of international operations at Lendlease, and features the Elephant and Castle redevelopment prominently, giving

Lendlease great advertising copy for its developments in the area.[11] A parallel trend is the growing interest among academic institutions in paid 'consultancy'. For example, the London School of Economics collaborated with housebuilders Berkeley to jointly publish 'New London Villages', a report which echoes the language of the pro-estate demolition lobby. A close look at the small print on the LSE website reveals, at the very bottom of the page, that the study was 'commissioned via LSE Consulting', part of LSE Enterprise, the 'global business arm' of LSE. But the Berkeley Group's own press release on the report mentions no such thing, claiming instead that the research is published by the LSE and Berkeley, with the housebuilder therefore gaining considerable academic credibility for themselves and the findings in the process.[12]

Across the West, the failures of the mainstream media, particularly in the UK and America, to report accurately on a wide range of issues, and the denigration of experts and evidence, have led to the coining of the phrase 'post-truth politics', and strategies to combat this must be at the heart of attempts to renew democracy. A blueprint for democratic renewal in public life, in government and in institutions is beyond the scope of this book, but as the housing crisis reaches a tipping point, it seems possible that political pressure from a new alliance of lower- and middle-income groups may create a more favourable climate for broader democratic renewal and certainly for a profound reworking of the housing paradigm in the UK. This is happening in cities across Europe, from Barcelona to Berlin, and among civil society groups in North America. What these changes – many of which are already successfully pursued in other parts of the world – could look like is the subject of the next section.

ALTERNATIVES

Imagine detaching your balcony from your flat, floating it on a canal, piloting it along the water around to your friend's house – with the chairs, tables, plants still on it – sailing both your floating balconies out to the harbour, tying them together and then swimming off them or having a party. Crazy? Only for the rich? No, it's something any-one living in the new flats in the Sluseholmen area of Copenhagen can do, where rents are reasonably priced and the new community is gen-uinely mixed. Or take DeFlat in Amsterdam, where local people are doing up hundreds of flats in a 1970s social housing complex con-demned for demolition. Two thirds of the buyers are from the local area or wider Amsterdam and the majority are on modest incomes and eligible for affordable housing. How about Vienna, where the city's tradition of high-quality public housing means that 50 per cent of the population live in beautifully built and well-maintained social homes, knit into a pattern of provision which includes libraries, kin-dergartens, day-care facilities and courtyard parks. Or take the Laituri Information and Exhibition Centre in the centre of Helsinki, which holds permanent and temporary exhibitions about the city's planned, ongoing and completed development projects, and provides three names and email addresses to show who is responsible for each project. Their map-based citizen survey garnered 33,000 comments and a municipal 'Urban Facts' department reports on all of this data and publishes it in an unusually honest quarterly magazine.

Claire Bennie is an architect who spent a decade as director of development at the Peabody Trust, one of the UK's best-known and well-regarded housing associations, which has been building housing for people on lower incomes since the nineteenth century. In 2015 she decided to spend two months travelling around ten countries in mainland Europe, looking at how and why they do things differently – and better. 'One reaction I got when I said I was from London was that people said, "oh, it's so sad what's happening there, it's just a paper chase, no one can afford it",' she told me. That was the view from Berlin, where city officials are introducing a range of measures which would be unthinkable in the UK in a specific bid to prevent Berlin becoming like London. In this, Berlin is helped by a new legis-lative renting framework for inner-city areas introduced by the German government in 2015, ensuring landlords are able to raise rents by only 10 per cent above the average for similar properties in a local area. Berlin, where 90 per cent of the population rent, was the first city to introduce the changes and since then other German states, including Hamburg and Bavaria, have followed suit.[13] Imagine that happening in London, where Sadiq Khan's main intervention with regards to gentrification is to commission a research report. In Berlin thirty-three districts have been designated 'urban conservation areas' where expensive redevelopments are banned, and in 2016, the city government successfully used an obscure legal tool known as a 'pre-emptive right of purchase' to prevent the sale of an apartment block in trendy Kreuzberg to an offshore company. As well as taking on Airbnb the city government is looking at a number of tax measures to cool foreign investment; it is considering imposing a tax on second homes which remain empty and it is monitoring closely the impact of Vancouver's new 15 per cent tax on foreign investors buying properties.[14] London, on the other hand, has one of the most generous tax regimes in the world for foreign investors.

One of the conclusions Bennie brought home was that the more equitable policies and practices she witnessed in Europe were not just a question of governance and politics but human interaction. 'We imagine in the UK that human nature is acquisitive and property-oriented – a door we shut that no one else will walk through. But that's a very American, Western-facing view. What amazed me in mainland Europe is that people are far more willing, able and culturally brought up to share – whether that's sticking a bench in front of your house and letting people sit on it who have nothing to do with you, which is fine in Holland, or the fact that all new housing in Helsinki has a communal sauna on every staircase.' This culture of sharing extends to sharing places with people on a variety of incomes, introduced either through Berlin's municipal measures or the standard development of genuinely mixed communities: 'Routinely there was 50 per cent affordable housing in all the developments I saw – of course it's all in the definition of affordable housing but that means 50 per cent subsidized housing,' she said. And they do not have the infamous 'poor doors', where tenants in social housing have vastly inferior entrances in sub-optimal places in alleyways, or near the bins.

Bennie singles out the UK's planning system as the main place we need reform and contrasts it with planning in Europe. 'There's something rotten about the contract in planning. It should determine the way land is mediated so that it benefits us all,' she said. Instead 'the pendulum has swung too far off' and rather than the social contract it should be, planning has become an 'obscure, legalistic and specialized activity, "practised" by suits and fought over largely behind closed doors', leading to the scandal of secret financial viability assessments engineered to provide no affordable housing. The other crucial difference is that municipal governments in Europe have greater power and financial backing, through mechanisms which create large pots of public money to kick-start European-style developments. In contrast, government in England is very highly centralized and local authorities no longer have the resources or the confidence to initiate large-scale projects. Instead, they act as enablers for the private sector, with public money used to lever in private sector development which then assumes the lead and takes ownership of places.

Rewriting the social contract with regard to property and planning is the biggest challenge we face in order to address the housing crisis. We also need to determine the role of the state in subsidizing people in housing need. The marketized housing benefit system is leading to a dangerously inflationary market that utterly fails the people it is designed to help. But there is no political will to move to a supply-based system and build the numbers of social and genuinely affordable homes people need. Instead, politicians continue to stick to the line that housebuilders will build more if only the planning system is loosened yet further, and that this is the way to solve the housing crisis, even though the new homes built over the last decade have not resulted in any more home ownership or affordable housing. Housing in the UK is dominated by the speculative model practised by the big housebuilders and an unregulated private rental market. As housebuilders are listed companies, whose first duty is to create profits for their shareholders, it is not surprising that they build up large land banks and 'trickle out' homes to increase profits rather than meet demand, while the dominant drive for the bottom line is reflected in the scandal of 'financial viablility assessments' that fail to provide any affordable housing at all.

Chris Brown, chief executive of the sustainable property invest-ment fund Igloo Regeneration, has advised government and works closely with the government's Homes and Communities Agency and the Greater London Authority. He highlights two key factors behind the housebuilders' approach. 'There is weak governance in the quoted companies. Managers are able to extract above market returns for their labour and the management of the big housebuild-ers stand to make a huge amount of money. The second issue is that they are not businesses with a purpose – but they could be. They could say our business is to house the nation but that would mean changing their business model.' Brown believes that in the UK today companies can be divided into those which are 'for profit and for purpose' and 'evil capitalists' out for themselves, with no concern for wider society. 'There are many companies trying to make the world a better place, which believe that is also good for businesss,' he said, citing Unilever and Legal & General. In his view the monopoly housebuilders belong to the other group.

But the crisis is not just limited to the housebuilders, it's systemic, with almost insurmountable barriers to change for alternative mod-els permeating every layer of government. In many other countries 'self-build', where owners build their own homes, is the main way new homes are created. Despite enthusiasm from local people and government this hasn't taken off in the UK. 'I'm trying to argue with government that they need a revolving fund to buy land for commu-nities, but there's no one in there who has any understanding of this,' Brown claimed. The commonly held view is that it's the price of land which inhibits smaller players from entering the market, and this is certainly of vital importance, but another significant barrier is that only those on an 'approved list' are allowed by local authorities to develop land and becoming a registered provider is no mean feat. As for local authorities, even when they might wish to work according to a different model with smaller players, they are under unprece-dented financial pressure. The examples of good practice from Europe, where the public sector is better skilled and better resourced, have been nurtured in a very different context from the UK. With the Brexit vote the emphasis on the private sector will probably be amplified and it is likely that London will continue with a tax regime favouring foreign investment, alongside policies towards affordable housing and the capping of benefits that will accelerate the removal of lower- and middle-income earners from the city. Even so, while the paradigm shift around planning and the benefits system is unlikely to happen any time soon without sustained and mounting pressure, the scale of the crisis is beginning to elicit a response, with the government indicating that it will not tolerate the worst excesses of the housebuilders any more. This was reflected in the Housing White Paper in 2017 which did express the desire to see a greater number of smaller sites made available for small and medium-sized builders, and cut from three years to two the length of time housebuilders are allowed to hold on to land without building on it – albeit with caveats.

Taking on the housebuilders in a meaningful way also involves looking at the range of tax inducements which accompany the speculative house building model. While this would require the same shift in political culture needed to rewrite the social contract with regard to planning, there is some comfort to be drawn from the growing and unlikely alliance of policymakers and campaigners beginning to make common cause around these issues. Top of the list is the need for a development land tax to recoup rising land values and keep markets under control, championed by luminaries from Adam Smith and Lloyd George to Churchill. This has been investigated and recommended by government inquiry after government inquiry.* It is part of the system in countries including Denmark, Singapore, Hong Kong and parts of the US and Australia, which are hardly bastions of socialism but which are prepared to intervene in property markets to safeguard decent housing. And it is a view shared by John Muellbauer, Professor of Economics at Oxford, who argues that a land value tax could play a part in stabilizing house prices. Politicians as diverse as the former Conservative planning minister Nicholas Boles and Green MP Caroline Lucas have made the case for it.[15] But despite the ongoing discussion the government has not

---

* The 2011 Mirrlees Review of the UK tax system argued that 'the economic case for taxing land itself is very strong'.

made any serious attempt to study its feasibility.* Given the inertia, the emerging political alliance around the housing crisis across income groups, in civil society and among some politicians needs to make this a priority.

On a smaller scale there is growing discussion about the role of Community Land Trusts, which sit outside the speculative model and depend on the community ownership of land, with the price of homes linked to local earnings. These also depend on the availability of affordable land and the willingness of local authorities to assist local groups who invest a huge amount of time and energy in getting these projects off the ground. Community Land Trusts now account for a significant part of the debate about how to solve the housing crisis, but so far they have played a very small part in actually doing so. When plans for the Olympic Park were first mooted self-build was touted as being a big part of the affordable housing planned for the area, alongside a Community Land Trust in the park, but in the end those plans were quietly dropped and the drive to obtain high land values reigned supreme. Today, there is one Community Land Trust of twenty-three homes in Mile End in East London with more planned, and a total of 225 trusts in England and Wales, but there is increasing interest in the model and indications that it is beginning to take off.

There are signs that some councils are starting to look at self-build. Brighton Council is piloting a project to identify difficult sites which do not appeal to larger developers and to allow self-build cooperative housing projects to take them over. So far eight sites have been identified, with more estimated to exist on the fringes of the city, and building is expected to start on the first one in 2017, after financing was obtained through loan stock offered by other cooperatives. Making it clear just how important the role of the council has been, Martyn, a co-op member and self-builder involved with the first project, said: 'It's a lot to do with having the land and the council being

---

* Also of vital importance is the exempting of VAT on newbuild but ensuring 20 per cent of it is paid on refurbishment. Alterations to this system, which would be vociferously resisted by developers, would do a lot to change the rush towards the demolition of London's housing estates.

prepared to help us.' In Leeds, LILAC is an ecological co-housing project selected as finalist in the World Habitat Awards, which are run in partnership with UN-Habitat. These are small-scale development projects which are managing to create new templates, with the emergence of a growing group of more ethical developers and architects, working in tandem with local communities and councils prepared to look at alternatives. Raphael Lee, an architect on the Brighton self-build scheme, concedes this is a drop in the ocean compared to the strength of self-build in Germany or cooperative housing in Scandinavia, but from his perspective, in contrast with most of the work he does, 'even this one project is inspirational'. Listening to him describe his experience of working with the self-builders felt like watching someone emerge blinking from a dark room into the sunlight: 'It means we can have conversations outside the commercial environment. We were able to design a home they wanted to live in. Just having one pocket like this is extraordinary because the machine is so huge and it's not just driven by some corrupt politicians, it's driven by all of us.'

Chris Brown believes there is huge appetite and demand for change and that 'if you removed the barriers this sector would grow massively'. He is working with a number of community groups to help them become developers themselves. For example, in Bermondsey in Southwark, the Leathermarket Community Benefit Society has a programme of building genuinely affordable housing on what have been identified as 'infill sites' on their estates. This means that rather than knocking down estates the number of homes can be increased through 'infill', with the result that the area has 'none of the social cleansing of the worst of the comprehensive demolition approaches'. By also addressing the need for more homes, infill is an approach which could offer an alternative to demolition if rolled out more widely. But it is not going to be easy.

Central Hill is another estate in Lambeth where campaigners have been fighting for infill rather than demolition. Designed by Rosemary Stjernstedt in 1963, under the leadership of Ted Hollamby, the chief architect at Lambeth, who believed that architecture was 'social art', the estate was designed to preserve the skyline and was carefully landscaped around existing trees and contours. Set in a stunning location just down from Gipsy Hill, with panoramic views across London, Central Hill has fought a battle on two fronts: to gain listed status and to persuade the council to look at its alternative plan for infill developed by Architects for Social Housing, in consultation with the community. Geraldine Dening from ASH showed me around, pointing out the wonderful views and the high land values, while we discussed the council's claims that it can't afford to refurbish the homes and that demolition is the only way to increase density. The ASH plan would raise revenue to repair the homes from existing rents and from the sale of some of the additional 230 new homes they would build which would not fundamentally change the architectural plan. Instead, the council intend to demolish the place entirely, creating a very different type of development in its place, albeit one that would include more homes overall.

Central Hill failed in its application to be given listed status and Lambeth agreed plans to demolish it, despite the campaign of widespread opposition. In the 2016 election for the local Gipsy Hill ward, there was a 32 per cent swing to the Green candidate, who opposed demolition, and who lost to Labour by just thirty-six votes. Despite the rush to demolition, the success of the legal battles of the Aylesbury residents reflects a wider shift in public opinion with regard to London's housing estates, even if that is not shared by local councils and the housing industry. The success of DeFlat in Amsterdam, which is mirrored by many other modernist housing schemes, is not limited to continental Europe but can also be seen in the clutch of modernist estates that have been listed in the UK, which include Byker in Newcastle, Park Hill in Sheffield, Goldfinger's Trellick Tower and Balfron Tower and Lubetkin's Hallfield Estate in London. It's no surprise to find that the Hallfield Estate and Balfron Tower have been largely repurposed into trendy, expensive apartments with many of the original residents long gone, but it does at least reveal how popular these modernist estates can be.

Another architect who worked under Ted Hollamby at Lambeth in the 1960s is Kate Macintosh, who also went on to design a dramatically landscaped estate, Dawson's Heights in Southwark. I first met Kate in 2015 when I took part in a gloomy debate on the housing crisis at which she was also speaking and where all the speakers referred to the demolition of London's estates. But the next time I saw Kate was at a very different occasion hosted by residents of a housing development she had built for older people in Lambeth which had just won listed status, following a fierce battle by the residents to save their homes. The multi-generational party – so different from the sort of housing events I've been used to attending – was also an opportunity to celebrate Kate herself as the residents had decided to rename the development 'Macintosh Court'. And then came the shock decision of the public inquiry into the compulsory purchase of homes on the Aylesbury, to reject Southwark Council's proposals. This does not mean that the demolition plans are over but it sends a sharp signal that residents cannot simply be ignored and paid pitiful amounts in compensation for their homes.

It is impossible to predict the future of the property economy in London, the UK and globally, as it could be damaged or boosted by the changing political context here and around the world. Perhaps it is helpful to look at addressing the housing crisis on different levels of scale: as a global, national and local issue. The paradigm shift which requires a new social contract to control foreign investment and fix the broken planning system, housing market and benefits system, is surely the long-term goal in the UK. But in the short term many, many communities are coming together, finding a voice and engaging politically to safeguard the idea that London is a place where people of all incomes and backgrounds can afford to live in mixed communities. This struggle for the right to the city, also taking place in many other cities, is in turn feeding into a broader struggle for democratic participation in local and national politics, which itself creates fertile ground for a shift in political culture. All across the West, in the US, Europe and the UK, politics is changing and while nobody can know what the outcome will be, there is no doubt that the speculation in property, land and housing underpinning today's global economy – and the threat that poses to the right to the city – will be at the centre of it.

Notes

I. BIG CAPITAL

1. 'Paradise lost: ending the UK's role as a safe haven for corrupt individuals, their allies and assets', Transparency International, April 2016
2. 'London property: a top destination for money launderers', Transparency International, December 2016
3. Evans, Judith, 'How laundered money shapes London's property market', *Financial Times*, 6 April 2016
4. Watts, Peter, 'The battle for Brompton Road Tube: the story of a ghost station', *The London Magazine*, 28 May 2014
5. Caesar, Ed, 'House of secrets: who owns London's most expensive mansion?', *The New Yorker*, 1 June 2015
6. Interview with Kensington estate agent, 14 September 2016
7. 'Faulty Towers: Understanding the Impact of Overseas Corruption on the London Property Market', Transparency International UK, March 2017
8. Wiles, Will, 'The crash boom and vulture urbanism: how the super-rich bailed out London, and what it cost us', unpublished University of East London MRes essay, 2016
9. Tobin, Lucy, 'The French love an iBath, Americans require a wet room for pets and the Russians need a panic pod . . . enter the London flash pads', *Evening Standard*, 3 October 2014
10. Email from Lauren Awcock, London Central Portfolio, 9 November 2016
11. Glucksberg, Luna, 'A view from the top: unpacking capital flows and foreign investment in prime London,' *City*, 20 (2), pp. 238–55, 2016. This paper is part of 'Life in the Alpha Territory', an ESRC-funded academic study led by Goldsmiths University, York University, Kings College London and the LSE. The study takes its name from the

geodemographic marketing data provided by data company Experian's classification system.

12. Ibid.

13. 'Global Power Brokers' – Experian Marketing Services, http://guides.businessstrategies.co.uk/mosaicuk2009/data/mosaicuk/pdfs/portraits/type1.pdf

14. *Sunday Times* Rich List 2016, 24 April 2016

15. 'The Distributional Effects of Asset Purchases', Bank of England, 12 July 2012, http://www.bankofengland.co.uk/publications/Documents/news/2012/nr073.pdf

16. 'The Wealth Report', 10th edition, Knight Frank, 2016, http://www.knightfrank.com/wealthreport

17. Ibid.

18. Lock, Grant, 'Digging deep: RBKC to undermine stability of Basement Permitted Development Rights?', Nathaniel Lichfield & Partners, 20 May 2015, http://nlpplanning.com/blog/digging-deep-rbkc-to-undermine-stability-of-basement-permitted-development-rights/

19. Shaxson, Nicholas, *Treasure Islands: Tax Havens and the Men who Stole the World*, Vintage, 2012

20. Butler, Tim and Lees, Loretta, 'Super-gentrification in Barnsbury, London: globalization and gentrifying global elites at the neighbourhood level', *Transactions of the Institute of British Geographers*, Vol. 31, Issue 4, pp. 467–87, December 2006

21. Glucksberg, 'A view from the top'

22. Atkinson, R., Burrows, R. and Rhodes, D., 'Capital city? London's housing market and the "super rich"', in I. Hay and J. Beaverstock (eds.), *International Handbook of Wealth and the Super Rich*, pp. 225–43, Edward Elgar, 2016

23. Madden, David and Marcuse, Peter, *In Defense of Housing: The Politics of Crisis*, Verso, 2016

24. Glucksberg, 'A view from the top'

25. 'Supercars crackdown success. The Royal Borough of Kensington and Chelsea', Newsroom press release, 28 July 2016, https://www.rbkc.gov.uk/press-release/supercars-crackdown-success

26. Fishwick, Samuel, 'This is what it's like to party with the Rich Kids of London', *ES Magazine*, 28 July 2016

27. Phillips, Tom, ' "This is just the start": China's passion for foreign property', *Guardian*, 29 September 2016

28. Moore, Rowan, *Slow Burn City*, Picador, 2016

29. MIPIM UK 2015: Conference & Event Programme, Wednesday 21 October 2015. Quoted in Minton, Anna, 'Developers at London's property fair are plotting how to demolish our homes', *Guardian*, 21 October 2015
30. Moore, *Slow Burn City*

2. THE FINANCIALIZATION OF HOUSING AND PLANNING

1. BBC, 'On this Day – 20 December 1979: Council tenants will have "right to buy"'
2. House of Commons Library Welfare Expenditure and Savings Tool (WEST), selecting 'Housing Benefit', 'Updated' and 'BE & C tables' options
3. Graham, Stephen, *Vertical*, Verso, 2016
4. Carlyon, Tristan, 'Food for thought: applying house price inflation to grocery prices', Shelter, February 2013
5. 'Eurostat Statistics Explained. Housing Statistics', http://ec.europa.eu/eurostat/statistics-explained/index.php/Housing_statistics
6. 'Expert Committee on Compensation and Betterment: Final Report, 1942, Great Britain, Ministry of Works and Planning', Sir Augustus Andrewes Uthwatt, HMSO, 1942
7. Colenutt, Bob, 'The viability attack on social and affordable housing. FOReTHOUGHT: Making Space for planning', research blog from the Department of Urban Studies and Planning at the University of Sheffield, 2 June 2015, http://sheffield-planning.org/2015/06/02/the-viability-attack-on-social-and-affordable-housing/
8. Flynn, Jerry, 'Complete control: developers, financial viability and regeneration at the Elephant & Castle', *City*, Vol. 20 (2), pp. 278–86, 2016
9. http://35percent.org/2013-07-30-how-to-avoid-providing-affordable-housing-a-guide-for-developers/
10. Roberts-Hughes, Rebecca, 'The case for space', RIBA, 2011
11. Till, Jeremy, Presentation to Central St Martin's one-day symposium, 'sensingsite – In this Neck of the Woods', 4 June 2015
12. Valentine, Daniel, 'Solving the housing crisis: an analysis of the investment demand behind the UK's housing affordability crisis', The Bow Group, November 2015
13. Valentine, Daniel, 'Building more houses won't bring down prices', politics.co.uk, 23 November 2015, http://www.politics.co.uk/

comment-analysis/2015/11/23/comment-building-more-houses-wont-bring-down-prices

14. Watt, Paul and Minton, Anna, 'London's housing crisis and its activisms', *City*, Vol. 20 (2), pp. 204–21, 2016

15. Minton, Anna, *Ground Control: Fear and Happiness in the twenty-first century City*, Penguin, 2009 (2012)

16. Barker, Kate, 'Review of Housing Supply. Final Report – Recommendations', HMSO, 2004

17. Ruddick, Graham, 'Revealed: housebuilders sitting on 450,000 plots of undeveloped land', *Guardian*, 30 December 2015

18. Youde, Kate, 'Home builders reject Miliband's land banking accusation', *Inside Housing*, 25 September 2014

19. Javid, Sajid, 'Building the homes we need', Speech to National Home Building Council, 24 November 2016

20. Local Government Association, 'Starter Homes and the extension of Right to Buy', House of Lords short debate, 22 February 2016

21. 'Research reveals scale of developers' profits', Centre for Regional and Economic Social Research, Sheffield Hallam University, 16 November 2016

22. Ibid.

23. Bate, Alex, 'Building the new private rented sector: issues and prospects (England)', House of Commons Library briefing paper, Number 07094, 12 December 2016

24. Jeraj, Samir and Walker, Rosie, *The Rent Trap*, Left Book Club, 2016

25. Bate, 'Building the new private rented sector'

26. 'World Student Housing: Class of its Own', Savills World Research, 2016–17

27. 'Lambeth Council Estate Regeneration: Homes for Lambeth', www.estateregeneration.lambeth.gov.uk/hfl/

28. Sender, Henry, 'Investment strategy: the new property barons', *Financial Times*, 3 April 2016

29. Beswick, Joe, Alexandri, Georgia, Byrne, Michael, Vives-Miró, Sònia, Fields, Desiree, Hodkinson, Stuart and Janoschka, Michael, 'Speculating on London's housing future: the rise of global corporate landlords in "post-crisis" urban landscapes', *City*, Vol. 20 (2), pp. 321–41, 2016

30. Ibid.

31. Dowsett, Sonya, 'Special Report – Why Madrid's poor fear Goldman Sachs and Blackstone', Reuters, 30 June 2014

32. Kerslake, Bob, 'Leading government figures see social housing as toxic', *Guardian*, 5 May 2016

33. 'The likely impact of the lower overall benefit cap', Chartered Institute of Housing, 1 November 2016

34. Watt and Minton, 'London's housing crisis and its activisms'

35. Perraudin, Frances, 'Government criticised for holding housing bill debate lasting until 2 am', *Guardian*, 6 January 2016

36. Topple, Steve, 'The Housing and Planning Bill reveals how little Tory MPs think of the public', *Independent*, 13 January 2016

3. DEMOLITIONS

1. Lees, Loretta, 'The urban injustices of New Labour's "new urban renewal": the case of the Aylesbury Estate in London', *Antipode*, 2013

2. 'Faulty Towers: Understanding the Impact of Overseas Corruption on the London Property Market', Transparency International UK, March 2017

3. 'Knock It Down or Do It Up? The Challenge of Estate Regeneration', London Assembly Housing Committee, February 2015. The report showed that between 2005 and 2015 around fifty estates with over 30,000 homes were subject to estate regeneration schemes which almost doubled the number of homes and increased the number of private homes tenfold but simultaneously entailed a net loss of 8,000 social rented homes.

4. Adonis, Andrew and Davies, Bill (eds.), 'City Villages: More Homes, Better Communities', Institute for Public Policy Research, 2015

5. 'New Homes for Heygate. Heygate Residents Rehousing Pack', Southwark Council, 2004. Available to view at: http://heygate-washome.org/displacement.html

6. Loretta Lees, Just Space and Southwark Notes Archive Group, 'Staying Put: An Anti-Gentrification Handbook for Council Estates in London', London Tenants Federation, 2014

7. Analysis of Freedom of Information requests, Heygatewashome.org, http://heygatewashome.org/displacement.html

8. Bar-Hillel, Mira, 'Elephant and Castle estate revamp "ripped off taxpayers"', *Evening Standard*, 6 February 2013

9. Minton, Anna, 'Scaring the living daylights: the local lobby and the failure of democracy', SpinWatch, 2013

10. 'Knock It Down or Do It Up?'

11. Lees, Loretta, Slater, Tom and Wyly, Elvin, *Gentrification*, Routledge, 2008

12. Lees, 'The urban injustices of New Labour's "urban renewal"'

13. Lees, Slater and Wyly, *Gentrification*

14. Minton, 'Scaring the living daylights'
15. Moore, Keith, 'Muggers' "paradise", the Heygate Estate is demolished', *BBC News London*, 15 April 2011
16. Aylesbury Estate Freedom of Information request dated 1 March 2016, Southwark Council
17. Campkin, Ben, *Remaking London: Decline and Regeneration in Urban Culture*, IB Tauris, 2013
18. Jacobs, Jane M. and Lees, Loretta, 'Defensible space on the move: revisiting the urban geography of Alice Coleman', *International Journal of Urban and Regional Research*. Vol. 37 (5), pp. 1559–83, 2013
19. Minton, Anna and Aked, Jody, 'Fortress Britain: high security, insecurity and the challenge of preventing harm', Prevention working paper, New Economics Foundation, 2013
20. '2011 London riots location analysis: proximity to town centres and post-war housing estates', Space Syntax, 2011
21. Campkin, *Remaking London*
22. Fletcher, Martin, 'Demolition of the Aylesbury Estate: dawn for hell's waiting room?', *The Times*, 20 October 2008
23. Campkin, *Remaking London*
24. Allen, Kate and Pickard, Jim, 'London councils urged to demolish and redevelop council estates', *Financial Times*, 22 March 2015
25. Smith, Neil, 'Gentrification and the rent gap', *Annals of the Association of American Geographers*, Vol. 77 (3), pp. 462–5, 1987
26. Watt, Paul, ' "It's not for us": regeneration, the 2012 Olympics and the gentrification of East London', *City*, Vol. 17 (1), pp. 99–118, 2013
27. 'Homes for Londoners. Draft Good Practice Guide to Estate Regeneration', Mayor of London, GLA, December 2016
28. 'The People's Plan: Cressingham Gardens Estate', 2016, https://moderngov.lambeth.gov.uk/documents/s80088/Appendix%20J%20-%20 Peoples%20Plan%20-%20Part%201.pdf
29. SAVE Britain's Heritage, Letter of Objection to Lambeth Council, 10 July 2015
30. 'Cressingham Gardens Estate', Social Life, 2015, http://www.social-life.co/media/files/FINAL_Exhibition_boards.pdf
31. 'High Court grants permission for legal action to London resident over redevelopment plans', press release by Leigh Day, 17 July 2015
32. 'Gamekeepers turned poachers. Better Elephant', 19 October 2014, http://betterelephant.github.io/blog/2014/10/19/gamekeepers-turned-poachers/

33. House of Commons Select Committee on Public Administration, Minutes of Evidence, Supplementary Memorandum by Defend Council Housing (CVP 05 (a))

34. Minton, 'Scaring the living daylights'

35. *You've Been Trumped*, dir. Anthony Baxter, BBC, 23 October 2012. Available from: www.you'vebeentrumped.com

36. Interview with Martyn Holmes, 13 January 2017

37. Commercial Lobbyists (Registration and Code of Conduct) Bill, House of Commons, 1 February 2013

38. Minton, 'Scaring the living daylights'

39. Douglas, Pam and Parkes, Joanne, ' "Regeneration" and "consultation" at a Lambeth council estate: the case of Cressingham Gardens', *City* Vol. 20 (2), pp. 287–91, 2016

40. Chakrabortty, Aditya and Robinson-Tillett, Sophie, 'The truth about gentrification: regeneration or con trick?', *Guardian*, 18 May 2014

4. FROM BRICKS TO BENEFITS

1. Watt, Paul, 'A nomadic war machine in the metropolis. Encountering London's 21st-century housing crisis with Focus E15', *City*, Vol. 20 (2), pp. 297–320, 2016

2. Ibid.

3. Wales, Robin, 'I apologise to the Focus E15 families, but this is a London housing crisis', *Guardian*, 6 October 2014

4. Focus E15 v Robin Wales and Newham Council, YouTube.com, https://www.youtube.com/watch?v=gsPxancNiqk

5. London Borough of Newham Decision Notice, attached in letter from Newham to Kevin Blowe regarding Complaint of breach of Members' Code of Conduct by the Mayor of Newham, 29 January 2015

6. Watt, 'A nomadic war machine in the metropolis'

7. Wainright, Oliver, 'London's Olympic legacy: a suburb on steroids, a cacophony of luxury stumps', *Guardian*, 3 August 2016

8. Theori Housing Management Ltd, Specialist Public Sector Services, http://theori.co.uk

9. 'Briefing: The growing Housing Benefit spend in the private rented sector', National Housing Federation, 20 August 2016

10. Watt, Paul and Minton, Anna, 'London's housing crisis and its activisms' *City*, Vol. 20 (2), 2016; 24 per cent of Londoners lived in social housing at the time of the 2011 census, a figure which is likely to be significantly lower today.

11. Ibid.

12. Aldridge, Hannah, Barry Born, Theo, Tinson, Adam and MacInnes, Tom, 'London's Poverty Profile', New Policy Institute, http://www.londonspovertyprofile.org.uk/key-facts/

13. Ibid.

14. Minton, Anna, *Ground Control: Fear and Happiness in the Twenty-first-century City*, Penguin, 2012

15. 'Editorial: Back in work, but still out of pocket', in *OECD Employment Outlook 2016*, OECD Publishing, Paris

16. Dixon, Ben, 'Tracking Welfare Reform: Local Housing Allowance an extended London Council's briefing', London Councils, 2013

17. Hopps, Kat, 'Newham's housing crisis is "only going to get worse" says council', *Newham Recorder*, 6 April 2016

18. Ibid.

19. Email correspondence with Greater London Authority official, 2016

20. Mungazi, Carl, *Luton on Sunday*, 1 August 2015

21. Nzolameso (Appellant) v City of Westminster. The Supreme Court. Case details. [2015] UKSC 22, 2 April 2015

22. Ibid.

23. 'Decision. Homelessness Policies. City of Westminster', 12 January 2017, http://westminster.moderngov.co.uk/ieDecisionDetails.aspx?ID=653

24. Hardy, Kate and Gillespie, Tom, 'Homelessness, health and housing. Participatory action research in East London', http://www.e15report.org.uk 2016

25. House of Commons Library Welfare Expenditure and Savings Tool (WEST), selecting 'Housing Benefit', 'Updated' and 'BE & C tables' options

26. 'London's Poverty Profile. Rough sleeping in London over time', New Policy Institute, 2016

27. Barnes, Sophie, 'Applicants barred by local connection rules', *Inside Housing*, 11 March 2016

28. Johnson, Andrew, 'Hammersmith and Fulham social housing register cut by nearly 90 per cent', *Conservative Home*, 5 April 2013, http://

www.conservativehome.com/localgovernment/2013/04/hammersmith-and-fulham-social-housing-register-cut-by-nearly-90.html

29. Webb, Kate, 'Bricks or benefits? How we can rebalance housing investment', Shelter, 2012

30. Watt and Minton, 'London's housing crisis and its activisms'

31. 'Housing Associations and Right to Buy', Communities and Local Government Select Committee Report, 10 February 2016

32. Live Tables on Rents, Lettings and Tenancies, https://www.gov.uk/government/statistical-data-sets/live-tables-on-rents-lettings-and-tenancies

33. HomeLet Rental Index, https://homelet.co.uk/homelet-rental-index/london

34. 'Housing Associations and Right to Buy'

35. 'Housing Benefit Millionaires', Channel 4, *Dispatches*, 14 March 2016

36. 'Evaluation of Removal of Spare Room Subsidy', Department for Work and Pensions, Final Report, 2015

37. 'Recent measures in the United Kingdom are eroding right to affordable housing – UN expert', UN News Centre, 11 September 2013

38. United Nations Human Rights, Country visits, United Kingdom of Great Britain and Northern Ireland (August–September 2013), 25th Session HRC, 2014, http://www.ohchr.org/EN/Issues/Housing/Pages/CountryVisits.aspx

39. 'Ministers criticise "partisan" UN housing report', *BBC News*, UK Politics, 3 February 2014

40. Seamark, Michael, 'Raquel Rolnik: a dabbler in witchcraft who offered an animal sacrifice to Marx', Mail Online, 12 September 2013

41. 'Under pressure: how councils are planning for future cuts', Local Government Association, 2014

5. GENERATION RENT

1. Minton, Anna, *Ground Control: Fear and Happiness in the Twenty-first century City*, Penguin, 2012

2. Jackson, Wayne, 'London Borough of Redbridge, Beds in Sheds Report, April 2013 – March 2015', 26 June 2015

3. 'Making a Slave', BBC iPlayer, http://www.bbc.co.uk/programmes/p043lx6n

4. 'Beds in Sheds and Rogue Landlords', Migrants' Rights Network, 2013

5. Lynch, Matthew, 'Estate agents offer illegal "beds in sheds" ', *BBC News*, 'Inside Out', London, 25 February 2013

6. 'Ending the tenant tax to help tackle rogue landlords', Department for Communities and Local Government, Press release, 12 May 2015

7. 'Are the government about to make it even harder to introduce selective licensing?', Shelter policy blog, 12 May 2015, http://blog.shelter.org.uk/2015/03/are-the-government-about-to-make-it-even-harder-to-introduce-selective-licensing/

8. Spurr, Heather, 'Clark vetoes council's PRS licensing scheme', *Inside Housing*, 23 December 2015

9. 'Housing in London 2017', London Datastore, GLA

10. Edwards, Michael, 'The housing crisis and London', *City*, Vol. 20 (2), pp. 222–37, 2016

11. 'What are renters thinking?', Briefing by Sian Berry, Green Party Member of the London Assembly, 2016

12. Skapinker, Michael, 'London house prices push out the people the city needs the most', *Financial Times*, 9 September 2015

13. Fifty Thousand Homes, 'London's housing crisis and what it means for business', http://www.fiftythousandhomes.london/facts/

14. Chakrabortty, Aditya, Keynote speech at 'London's Housing Crisis and its Activisms' one-day conference, hosted by the University of East London and Birkbeck College at University Square, Stratford, 26 April 2016

15. This conversation took place in spring 2016. In the summer Jane sold her flat.

16. Abbey, Ciaran and Balamurali, T.B.S., 'Housing the Mind', The Legatum Institute, 2016

17. Lees, Loretta and White, Hannah, 'Why We Can't Afford to Lose It: Local Authority Housing in London Protects the Poor from Homelessness', University of Leicester and Cambridge House report, in partnership with Lambeth County Court Duty Scheme, 2016

6. THE 'RIGHT TO THE CITY'

1. 'Prime London Residential Markets', Savills, January 2017

2. 'No "Kosovo-style cleansing" of poor, says Johnson', *BBC News*, 28 October 2010

3. Boris Johnson, Keynote speech at the first MIPIM London, 2014

4. Off the record interview with senior housing policy official, October 2016

5. James Murray, Keynote address to the London Real Estate Forum, 15 June 2016

6. PAH International Committee, pahinternacional website, 3 November 2016, http://afectadosporlahipoteca.com/2016/11/03/pah-international-committee/

7. Colau, Ada, 'After Habitat III: a stronger urban future must be based on the right to the city', *Guardian*, 20 October 2016

8. Minton, Anna, 'Scaring the living daylights out of people: the local lobby and the failure of democracy', SpinWatch, 2013

9. Ponsford, Dominic, '6,000 drop in number of UK journalists over two years – but 18,000 more PRs, Labour Force Survey shows', *Press Gazette*, 9 September 2015

10. Ford, Martin, 'Deciding the fate of a magical, wild place', *Journal of Irish and Scottish Studies*, Vol. 4 (2), 2011

11. Labbad, Dan, 'Smart urban regeneration projects put people and partnerships first', paid content, *Guardian*, 4 July 2016, https://www.theguardian.com/lendlease-redesigning-cities-zone/2016/jul/04/smart-urban-regeneration-projects-put-people-and-partnerships-first

12. 'Community is king: how new London villages can help solve the housing crisis', Berkeley Group Press Release, 22 July 2016, https://www.berkeleygroup.co.uk/press-releases/2016/how-new-london-villages-can-help-solve-the-housing-crisis

13. Carson, James, 'Rent controls: lessons from Berlin', *The Knowledge Exchange* blog, 6 May 2016, https://theknowledgeexchangeblog.com/2016/05/06/rent-controls-lessons-from-berlin/

14. Chazan, Guy, 'Germany: Berlin's war on gentrification', *Financial Times*, 10 October 2016

15. 'Land Value Taxation', House of Commons Library, 17 November 2014

Acknowledgements

My first thanks go to the 1851 Royal Commission for the Great Exhibition, which awarded me a two-year fellowship in the Built Environment in 2011, to enable me to continue my research and write a second book, to follow *Ground Control*. On *Big Capital* I was very lucky to work again with my editor Helen Conford and agent Karolina Sutton at Curtis Brown, ably assisted by the team at Penguin, Shoaib Rokadiya and Richard Duguid, and dedicated copy editor Bela Cunha. Photographer Henrietta Williams took the powerful and evocative images which accompany the text.

My fellowship coincided with the birth of our second son Daniel, and the 1851 was kind enough to stretch the fellowship over three years. During this time, I wrote a number of papers which informed *Big Capital*, including 'Common Good(s): Redefining the public interest and the common good', which was published by How to Work Together, a shared programme of contemporary art commissioning and research organized by Chisenhale Gallery, The Showroom and Studio Voltaire. This paper was the starting point for the research into the planning system which underpins chapter 2, and I would like to thank Chisenhale director Polly Staple for facilitating this. 'Scaring the living daylights: the local lobby and the failure of democracy' was published by Spinwatch and Tamasin Cave played a key role in helping to get this publication off the ground, which was vital to my work on the functioning, or otherwise, of local democracy. The third publication in this series, 'Fortress Britain', was published as a working paper by the New Economics Foundation. It looked at the importance of Secured by Design policy and deepened my understanding of the securitization of the urban environment and the 'sink estate' narrative discussed in chapter 3.

Big Capital crystallized in 2015, when I was invited by the Bristol Festival of Ideas to participate in a gloomy debate on the housing crisis with the celebrated modernist architect Kate Macintosh. Speaker after speaker got up to talk about the demolition of London's housing estates and the devastation caused to communities. When it came to Kate's turn, she spoke of the success of recent community projects in bringing North London's once troubled Broadwater Farm Estate together. Does she not know it's also under threat of demolition, I wondered to myself. It turns out she did, breaking down in tears at the thought of what the community now had to face, despite all their efforts. Then she composed herself and continued. But as she returned to her seat, she tripped up on a misplaced lead and fell, breaking her arm. It was an upsetting incident and felt to me like a disturbing metaphor for London's housing crisis. I went home feeling that it was necessary to combine my work so far with a specific investigation of the housing crisis.

At the same time, Bob Catterall, the editor of the brilliant multi-disciplinary journal *City*, had commissioned a Special Feature on the housing crisis, which I was co-editing with Paul Watt, Reader in Urban Studies at Birkbeck. I owe Paul a huge debt of gratitude for the work we did together on that Special Feature and the accompanying housing conference we hosted at the University of East London in spring 2016. All the papers in the Special Feature have informed the book; Michael Edwards on the financializaiton of housing, Luna Glucksberg on the 'alpha elites', Simon Elmer and Geraldine Dening from Architects for Social Housing on the 'London Clearances', Stuart Hodkinson on Global Corporate Landlords and Paul's own study of the role of the campaign group Focus E15, as well as the encyclopaedic account of past and present housing policy which he contributed to our co-authored introduction on 'London's housing crisis and its activisms'. Jerry Flynn's rigorous paper on financial viability in Elephant and Castle and the account by Pam Douglas and Joanne Parkes of events on Cressingham Gardens provided an important campaigning voice.

Many other academics have contributed to my understanding of the range of subjects related to the housing crisis and I would like to single out two in particular. Loretta Lees, professor of human geography at Leicester University, undertook research on the Aylesbury Estate and was the first to provide a forensic examination of the unfolding scandal. Loretta is now leading an ESRC-funded study into gentrification, displacement and council estate renewal which is certain to keep this issue on the agenda. Roger Burrows, professor of cities at Newcastle University's School of Architecture, Planning and Landscape, has been unfailingly generous in sharing with me his work and many papers on life in the 'alpha territory'. This two-year ESRC interdisciplinary study on the super-rich, which Luna Glucksberg contributed to, was led by Roger when he was at Goldsmiths, together with Caroline Knowles, in collaboration with Rowland Atkinson at York University, Tim Butler and Richard Webber at King's College London and Mike Savage at the LSE.

I would like to mention a number of my friends and colleagues at the School of Architecture at the University of East London. Alan Chandler, head of research for the school, and Professor Maria Segantini, director of C+S Architects, have consistently been very supportive of my work. And both of them offered practical help by providing me with offspring who wished to be my summer holiday researchers. Agnes Chandler did a fantastic job researching a complex aspect of housing benefit policy, which enabled me to make a key point about the unintended consequences of government policy. She also painstakingly compiled a list of council estates under threat. Marco Cappai was equally diligent, researching house price inflation in the UK and collating important historical and international comparisons. Carl Callaghan, the head of school, assisted the smooth running of the housing conference and Roland Karthaus, Bridget Snaith, Harald Trapp and Tony Fretton have all shared their ideas about urban policy and neoliberalism with me.

I would like to thank my MRes students in 2015 and 2016. The writing of the book coincided with the first two years of this new course on the neoliberal city, which has so far achieved that ideal situation where the students contribute to my work and vice versa.

Unpublished essays by last year's students Will Wiles, Toby Broadhurst and Chryssa Kanellakis-Reimer contributed to my thinking on media reporting of the property boom, the *banlieues* and the Aylesbury Estate. And two of my students, Nicolas Marchiaro and Martyn Holmes, make personal appearances in the book as a result of their experiences of the housing crisis.

I would also like to thank Jane Rendell, professor of architecture and art at the Bartlett, Peter Cosmetatos, who cast his eye over much of the manuscript, Kate Rosser for her help calculating property price inflation, Alberto Duman, who was Leverhulme Artist in Residence with the MRes in 2015–16, Dan Hancox, Geraldine Dening, Sian Berry, Chris Brown, Claire Bennie, Elaine Knutt, Andrea Eisenhart, Selina Mills, Cressida O'Shea and the campaign group 35 per cent who provide an invaluable research resource.

Most of all I would like to thank the people whose stories informed this book and who gave up their time to talk to me. Researching and writing the book was challenging because the worse the situation gets the greater the urgency to address it becomes. Ultimately, this is not a book about abstract-sounding housing and planning policies, it's about people's lives and what individuals, families and children have to endure as a result of the housing crisis, and for this reason the book is dedicated to them.

Of course, no thanks can be complete without mentioning my family. My partner, Martin Pickles, bore the brunt of childcare, and the extended family – my mum Helen Minton, my brother Aris Minton and Martin's parents, Dagmar and Chris Pickles – also helped enormously, as did Lorraine Varley. Thomas, who is six and a half, and Daniel, who is four, did not see their mum enough on many evenings and weekends when I was in the final stages of writing, but I hope that when they are older they will agree that it was worth it.

Index

Helsinki, 122, 123
Henry Jackson Society, 3
Heseltine, Lord, 67
Heygate Estate, Elephant and
    Castle, 24, 34–5, 37, 48–56
Heywood, Rachel, 74
'High Net Worth Individuals', 9
high rises ('streets in the sky'),
    25–7
Highgate, xi, 4–5, 11
Highgate Literary Society, 4
Highpoint, Highgate, 4
Hirst, Damien, 21
Hodkinson, Stuart, 45
Hollamby, Ted, 128–9
homelessness, 77–89
  'anti-homeless spikes', xii
  criminalization of, 113
  'hidden homeless', 90–91
  local councils' duties, 85, 86, 90
  and Right to Buy policies, 29
  in Spain, 116
Hong Kong, 9, 126
Horizon (BBC programme), 64
house prices, xii
  definitions of 'affordable',
    33–4, 48*
  and global capital flows, xvi, 5,
    6, 7, 14–15, 31, 41
  and increase of housing supply,
    xiv, 6–7, 36, 39–40, 68
  inflation of in UK, 30, 31, 41
  recent falls, 113
  and schools, 12
housebuilding
  in 1930s private sector, 41
  crisis as not market question of
    supply, xiv, 6–7, 36, 68
  deliberate limiting of supply,
    39, 40

increased profits for top five
    firms, xv–xvi, 41–2
  and 'land banking', 40,
    124, 126
  and market forces, 36–7, 39,
    40, 68
  monopoly of top
    housebuilders, 40
  policy from 1980s, xv, 27–30,
    31, 33–6
  postwar settlement, 25–7
  quality of homes, 36
  speculative market underpinning,
    8–9, 14, 21–2, 31, 36,
    113–14, 124, 126, 130
housing
  and 'alpha elites', xi–xii, 1–5, 8–9,
    10–19, 20–24
  banlieues in British cities, 90,
    107
  crisis as not market question of
    supply, xiv, 6–7, 36, 68
  'Exchange value' and 'use value', 7
  financialization of (from 1980s),
    29, 37–47
  'golden postcodes', xi–xii
  and human rights, xvi, 30, 60,
    62, 94
  ideal of property ownership,
    92, 102
  Sadiq Khan's 'London Living
    Rent', 115
  and May government, 42, 46
  Montague review, 42
  and neoliberal framework,
    xiv–xv, 62–3, 106–7
  privatization by stealth,
    37, 38
  property used purely as profit,
    xii–xiii, 6–7